SUNSET CARSON
The Adventures of a Cowboy Hero

by
Bobby J. Copeland
and
Richard B. Smith, III

Published by:

Empire Publishing, Inc.
3130 US Highway 220
Madison, NC 27025-8306

336-427-5850
www.empirepublishinginc.com

Other books by Bobby J. Copeland:
Trail Talk, published by Empire Publishing
B-Western Boot Hill, published by Empire Publishing
Bill Elliott — The Peaceable Man, published by Empire Publishing
Roy Barcroft — King of the Badmen, published by Empire Publishing
Charlie King — We Called Him Blackie, published by Empire Publishing
Silent Hoofbeats, published by Empire Publishing
Johnny Mack Brown — Up Close and Personal, published by Empire
    Publishing
The Bob Baker Story, published by BoJo Enterprises
The Whip Wilson Story, published by BoJo Enterprises
Five Heroes, published by BoJo Enterprises
The Tom Tyler Story (Mike Chapman and Bobby Copeland), published
    by Culture House Books
Best of the Badmen by Boyd Magers, Bob Nareau and Bobby Copeland,
    published by Empire Publishing
Smiley Burnette — We Called Him Frog, published by Empire Publishing

Empire Publishing, Inc.
3130 US Highway 220
Madison, NC 27025-8306
Phone: 336-427-5850
Fax: 336-427-7372
Email: info@empirepublishinginc.com

Library of Congress Catalog Number 2007938477
ISBN Number 978-0944019-52-8

Published and printed in the United States of America
1 2 3 4 5 5 6 7 8 9 10

SPECIAL THANKS TO THE FOLLOWING INDIVIDUALS

Paul Dellinger
Grady Franklin
Boyd Magers
Jerry Whittington
Bill Russell
Clint Mitchell
Les Adams
Lance Copeland
Tommy Scott
Minard Coons
Jim Hamby
Jim Martin
Jim Kocher
Bill Sasser
Ross Pittman
Joe Copeland
Paul Isenhour
Don Key
Sue Cannon
John Leonard
Merrill McCord

TABLE OF CONTENTS

SUNSET CARSON — FACT OR FICTION?

Sunset Carson told so many stories about his life and career that it's difficult to tell fact from fiction (much like the stories told about Tom Mix and Whip Wilson.) Of course, a lot of his claims were untrue, and over the years, fact and fiction merged until they became difficult to separate. As a result, the truth about Sunset's early years is elusive and shrouded with layers of myth. I have done extensive research on Sunset, and have drawn my own conclusions, and present here what my research has revealed.

Sunset Carson claimed various dates for his age: 1918, 1920, 1921, 1922, 1924, 1925, and finally 1927. He stated, on his Social Security application (dated June 30, 1937), that he was born in 1918 and that his name was Mickey Harrison. Apparently, he lied to make himself older (18) to better enable him to find employment. Regarding the other dates — one of his cousins, Jack Duffy, said, "Uncle Mick (his nephews always called him "Uncle Mick") was very vain about his age; he wanted people to think he was younger than he really was so he kept changing the dates." Duffy also told of Sunset having two daughters — one in Australia and another in California and a son who has since died.

Many times Sunset said he was born in Plainview, Texas. However, at one film festival he told he was born in Gracemont, Oklahoma. According to relatives, the Carson family moved from Gracemont to Plainview when Sunset was about eight years old.

(Actually, the family moved to the tiny community of Westside, which is closer to Olton, Texas, than it is to Plainview. The population of Olton was only around 2,200 some 80 years later. It is assumed Sunset claimed Plainview as home because it is larger than Olton.)

Also, Sunset often said his name was either Michael James Harrison, or Mickey James Harrison. The truth about this and some of his other statements were cleared up by what his mother wrote in her Bible (I think she should know). It confirms he was born on November 12, 1920, at Gracemont (Caddo County), Oklahoma, and his birth name was Winifred Maurice Harrison (his daughter, in California, said he never legally changed his name). Sunset's father was Maurice Greeley Harrison, and his mother was Azalee Belle "Dot" McAdams. His parents married in 1919.

Very little is known about Sunset's siblings, but he had a brother named Herman Dale Harrison (10/12/1923 - 1/7/2000) who appeared in three of Sunset's Yucca movies: SUNSET CARSON RIDES AGAIN (1947) and FIGHTING MUSTANG in 1948 (billed as Dale Harrison), and BATTLING MARSHAL in 1950 (billed as Dale Carson). Sunset also had three sisters — Azalee, Chloie and Peggy. One of Sunset's longtime girl friends told me Peggy was a former beauty queen who later developed polio.

(Sunset's sisters were at the Olton, Texas "Sunset Carson Day" celebration in 2005. Peggy was pictured in a motorized scooter.)

It has long been a mystery as to why Sunset left Republic before his scheduled picture deal was completed. He told two

Sunset at the Westside Grammar School near Olton, Texas. He is the tall boy on the back row with the unruly hair. He was about 10 at the time. Wonder if he was thinking of being a movie cowboy?

stories:
1. His agent told him he could do better elsewhere.
2. He did not know why Republic let him go.
According to the great stuntman, Yakima Canutt, Republic czar Herbert J. Yates threw a big party where all the studio's cowboy stars were expected to attend. Sunset showed up drunk and with an underage female. Yates had warned him before about some of his antics, and this time Sunset had gone too far. The irate Yates not only fired Sunset, but told him that he would see to it that no other studio hired him. Although Sunset was very popular at the time (ranked number eight among the top-ten moneymaking stars), Yates was successful in his threat because Sunset did not get work again until 1947, and then it was for the tiny Yucca Pictures under producer Walter Mattox. The four movies he made there were terrible and in no way matched the 15 exciting Republic entries. Sunset told me, "The pictures I made after leaving Republic weren't worth a dime."

Surprisingly, at one festival, Sunset praised Yates for the morality shown in Republic's Western films and for the standards he set for the cowboys regarding their personal appearances (not to be seen smoking, drinking, etc.).

According to Sunset, he dropped out of high school his sophomore year to join a rodeo. Did he win rodeo championships in South America as he claimed? Maybe, but there is little evidence to substantiate the claim. I suspect this story, like many of the tales about Tom Mix's life and the story of Buck Jones saving people from the Cocoanut Grove fire, is pure fabrication. The question immediately comes to my mind — with all the prestigious rodeos in the U. S. — why would he be participating in South America? Yet, there seems to be some evidence to support Sunset's claim: In an interview with leathercrafter Bob Brown, there is a newspaper clipping on Brown's wall about Sunset winning the All-Around Champion Cowboy of Argentina. And Brown displays the rope given to him by Sunset, which he supposedly used in the Argentina rodeo contests.

Sunset was married five times. On August 22, 1938, using his birth name Winifred M. Harrison, he married Patricia Eleanor Hussy in Yuma, Arizona. Although both listed California addresses, they probably married at Yuma because there was no waiting period in Arizona. The marriage produced a daughter, Ann Caleen Harrison, born March 29, 1940, in Vallejo, California. The marriage ended in divorce. He next married Betty Joyce Price (date unknown). A son Michael resulted from this union. After Betty divorced Sunset, she married Dr. Edward Johnson, an orthopedic surgeon. Dr. Johnson adopted Michael, who was four years old at the time, and raised him as his son. Betty died in 1993, and Dr. Johnson died in 2002. Michael died on November 16, 2003, as a result of a tractor accident on his farm in Autauga County, Alabama. He was 55 years old.

In 1953, Sunset was married briefly to Dorothy Shockley.

Sunset and son Michael with actress Susan Oliver.

Left to right: Sunset's girl friend, Jean; Sunset's 2nd wife, Betty Jo (mother of Michael), Sunset, and Betty Jo's new husband Dr. Edward Johnson.

He next marched down the aisle, this time as Michael Harrison, with Margaret J. Nesbitt on August 15, 1969. A daughter, Suzanne (thought to be living in Australia) was born of this marriage. Sunset said the daughter was born in Tasmania — not Australia as many have stated. Margaret already had a son by a previous marriage.

His final trip to the altar, using the name Mickey Harrison, was to Jeanne Jackson Davis, on June 17, 1989. It lasted less than a year due to Sunset's death on May 1, 1990. I mentioned to his cousin that I had seen Sunset at a film festival only a few weeks before his death, and that his faced was flushed, and he looked extremely fatigued. The cousin responded that Sunset and all of his siblings suffered from hypertension (high blood pressure).

There have been several persons who have fraudulently claimed to be certain movie or TV cowboys including ones for

Sunset with his last wife, Jeanne.

Bob Steele, Ken Maynard, Rocky Lane, Gabby Hayes, and Lee Aaker. There was also a man posing as Wild Bill Elliott Jr., which is interesting since Elliott had no sons. Two individuals have claimed to be Sunset Carson Jr. One of the impersonators was an obvious fake, and it is known that Sunset told him in no uncertain terms to cease and desist. The other person's claim seems more plausible.

In 2001, I made contact with a man who calls himself Sunset Carson Jr. He wrote, *I was born Jeffrey Paul Alexander in Los Angeles, California. My mother legally changed my name to Sunset Carson Jr. when I was six years old; this is what is on my passport. My mother Gloria Alexander was a script girl and an editor for Republic for many years. She was engaged to Sunset for a long time. She apparently broke up with him due to his violent temper and alcoholic behavior. I am a product of that relationship. I know about Sunset's other children. I have only corresponded with his son Michael twice in my life. Sunset's daughter refuses to talk with me. I understand after Sunset's funeral, there was a big fight over his belongings. I later went to Jeanne's (his widow) house to obtain some film I had shot with Sunset, and she gave me what she had. I do not think Sunset's family ever accepted Jeanne, which is why they tried to have his body relocated from the cemetery at Jackson, Tennessee.*

(Perhaps Alexander is an imposter, too, but his story rings true.)

Many critics have panned Sunset's acting ability including Don Miller, author of *Hollywood Corral*: *He was very young, very tall, and had a baby face that women cottoned to, and spoke slower than John Wayne, which was slow indeed, in a high-pitched voice. He also had to take second billing to Smiley Burnette, perhaps the first and only time in Western cinema history that a comic won the ace spot and the hero was second banana. No one would call Sunset Carson a great actor, but Peggy Stewart played their scenes together so as not to upstage him. Carson made strides as an action star, emphasis on action — his accomplishments consisted mainly of a likable smile and boyish mobility.*

Thomas Carr, who directed 10 of Sunset's movies, said, "I knew I had a cowboy on my hands that could not act, so I limited the dialogue and created as much action as I could for his pictures."

Alan G. Barbour, author of *Saturday Afternoon at the Movies* wrote: *It took some doing to make an actor out of the cowpoke. One story maintained that his delivery of lines was so bad (he ran them all together without pausing) that co-stars Tom London and Peggy Stewart actually painted a huge period on a piece of cardboard, and told Carson to stop every time they held it up out of camera range and count to four before he delivered his next line. If you look closely, you can see his lips moving slightly in some scenes as he did just that. But regardless of minor details like acting, Sunset was top notch in the action category, and that is what counted with the fans. It was easy to see why claims were made that he was getting more fan mail in the Southern states than Rogers or Autry.*

Sunset made only 15 features and one guest star appearance in Roy Rogers' BELLS OF ROSARITA (1945), but he was one of Republic's best received stars. The studio had started him out in films that top-billed Smiley Burnette, but Republic soon got rid of the comic, who off-screen was far from pleasant or amusing, and boosted Carson to the lead spot.

Peggy Stewart, a life-long friend and who worked with Sunset in these Republics: CODE OF THE PRAIRIE (1944), FIREBRANDS OF ARIZONA (1944), OREGON TRAIL (1945), and ROUGH RIDERS OF CHEYENNE (1945) said: "Tommy Carr (director) asked Tom London and I to please help out with Sunset. We did the best we could to help him improve his acting. He would run all his lines together. We taught him to pause between sentences."

(Note: This seems to confirm Barbour's story about the huge

period on the piece of cardboard.)

Perhaps author Les Adams best summed up Sunset's screen presence: *If it had been around 1924 for silent Westerns, Sunset Carson might have today been remembered as the best Western star of them all; he was tall, good looking and took second behind very few in riding, fighting and action ability. But it was 1944, and he was expected to know how to talk.*

I think Sunset's lack of thespian skills is exactly why he is so fondly remembered by Western fans today — the kids wanted action, and his films had little dialogue and were loaded with action.

After his screen career, Sunset made many personal appearances, including several Western film festivals. He really enjoyed his fans. Peggy Stewart said that Sunset lived to attend the festivals and mingle with his fans. He had numerous jobs, but apparently none of them lasted very long. Practically all the jobs were offered in an attempt to capitalize on his name.

Some of his endeavors include many appearances at promotions, jobs at Hillbilly World in Tennessee and other amusement parks, circuses, and the Tommy Scott Wild West Show where he replaced Tim McCoy. He even tried to launch an operation called Carson City, in North Carolina, which was to include appearances by surviving B-Western stars but, like many of his other enterprises, it was a failure.

One of his most bizarre appearances was on July 15, 1949, in Atlanta, Georgia, when Tom Mahoney "beat" Al Massey for the Southern Heavyweight Wrestling Title. Sunset was hired to be there and present the championship belt to the winner.

On many of his personal appearance engagements, Sunset put on a shooting exhibition. He was a crack shot and fans were amazed at his marksmanship. I was privileged to see his shooting exhibition in my hometown of Oak Ridge, Tennessee. This was around 1950, and he was with some small circus. His shooting exhibition, with a rifle, included extinguishing lighted candles, driving nails in boards, striking matches, popping balloons off people's head, and shooting cigarettes out of a performer's mouth.

Sunset's appearances were not limited to the United States. He took a worldwide tour and at least part of it was sponsored by the State Department. He visited Thailand where he gave a command performance before the King and Queen. I recall a story Sunset told me, and I think it happened in Thailand (now Siam), where he was giving his shooting demonstration, and the King wanted him to shoot a cigarette out of his mouth. The State Department representative told Sunset he could not do it due to what might happen to U. S. relations with the country in the event he accidentally shot the King. However, the King insisted he wanted it done. Sunset said, "I decided, since I was in the King's country, that he was the boss so I did it. "

From Thailand, he traveled to Hong Kong and appeared before various groups including a charity show for under-privileged children. His next stop was in the Philippines where he performed before the President and the First Lady. From there, he went to Formosa for a charity show for orphans and a command performance before Madame and Chiang Kai Shek. He then visited Okinawa, New Guinea, New Zealand and Australia. He final stop was in Tokyo where he did a series of charity events for victims of a typhoon. It was a long and rewarding trip for the

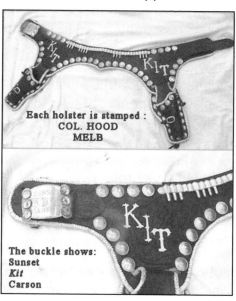

Each holster is stamped :
COL. HOOD
MELB

The buckle shows:
Sunset
Kit
Carson

Sunset on tour in Australia during the early 1950s.

cowboy star.

The Okinawa Morning Star said of Sunset: *Western Hero Sunset Carson has hit Okinawa with a bang, and is gaining the admiration of Ryukyuan kids as well as his loyal American fans. Unlike many cowboys, he is a sharpshooting Texan that handles his guns like a magician. He can practically split a hair with his rifle and is equally deadly with his pistols. He doesn't sing; he has no limping sidekick; he carries no cane; he carries no sawn-off shotgun; and his horse doesn't do the cha-cha, but if you catch his unusual act, you will agree he knows his way around the prairie.*

Before he began his successful PBS "Six Gun Heroes" television show, he had hosted another TV program in Hickory, North Carolina. Similar to "Six Gun Heroes," the show featured

Bad guys John Merton and Kenne Duncan are held at bay by Sunset Carson for this lobby card scene from OREGON TRAIL (Republic, 1945). Si Jenks is on far right with Peggy Stewart above Merton.

An unknown player and John Carpenter point their guns at a trapped Sunset Carson during THE EL PASO KID (Republic, 1946).

his movies and those of other Western stars.

Sunset, like Lash LaRue, became sort of a vagabond. The ladies were crazy about him, and his fans were delighted to have him spend time with them. As long as Sunset and Lash were roaming through the South, they could find brief employment or fans that would gladly have them as guests in their homes for a period of time. Sunset was extremely popular in the South, perhaps even more so than Gene Autry and Roy Rogers. The Southern folks accepted him as one of their own, and they related to his Texas drawl, simple country-boy charm, and they dearly loved his action-filled films.

Monte Hale described Sunset's popularity: "I'll tell you folks, when he was at Republic, Sunset was getting more fan mail than any of the other cowboys — even Roy Rogers. I saw the stacks of mail he used to get."

Sunset Carson ponders the concern of Linda Stirling prior to a robbery attempt in RIO GRANDE RAIDERS (Republic, 1946).

Anyone who ever met Sunset could readily tell he was not the "sharpest knife in the drawer." When he made a recording of recitations, he pronounced Joel McCrea's name as "Joel Mc-Cree," and Buster Crabbe's name "Buster Crab-be."

However, he was a very pleasant man, and he became one of the most popular guest stars to appear on the film festival circuit. Sunset enjoyed the adoration he received from his fans, and he did everything within his power to please them. He finally whipped the alcohol problem which had plagued him for so long. I never saw him drunk or "feeling good" at any of the festivals in the 1980s and 1990s.

Much credit should go to Sunset and Lash LaRue for the success of the Western film festivals. They were among the first cowboy stars to attend the festivals and, to the fans' delight, they became regulars on the festival circuit. It is unlikely these events would have enjoyed their long run without the appearances of Western screen personalities. Sunset and Lash led the way.

Although he was not in the same league with many of the highly touted cowboy stars like Buck Jones, Bill Elliott, Roy Rogers, William Boyd, Gene Autry, and several others, Sunset was a participant in our beloved B-Westerns, and he should be fondly remembered for his contribution.

If you want to see an exciting B-Western, pop in a video or DVD of one of his Republic movies, especially SANTA FE SADDLEMATES, THE CHEROKEE FLASH, or SHERIFF OF CIMARRON, all 1945 releases.

STAGE DOOR CANTEEN (United Artists, 1943). Left to right: Lon McCallister, Sunset (as Michael Harrison), Bill Terry, Fred Brady.

SUNSET SPEAKS

When we moved to Plainview, we lived so far from school that I had to ride a horse to school and carry my lunch, biscuits with bacon or ham and a bottle of milk, in my saddlebag. In the winter time, my milk would freeze and be practically like ice cream.

We lived on a dirt road about 21 miles from town. When it rained, the cars couldn't make it through the mud, so my brother and I would ride horses to town on Saturday to see the cowboy shows. We had two theaters, the Oneida and the Texas; one charged 10 cents and the other charged 12 cents. After watching the shows, we had to ride the 21 miles back home.

Even as a little kid, I wanted to be a movie cowboy. When I told my daddy this, he said that I should never start smoking because Tom Mix and those other cowboys didn't smoke, so I never smoked.

(Note: Apparently, Sunset's father never told him about the movie cowboys not drinking because alcohol caused him to not only lose his job at Republic, but several other job opportunities over the years. To his credit, in the later years of his life, he led a campaign to prevent children from partaking of drugs and alcohol.)

SUNSET CARSON
I SAID NO. SUNSET CLUB

I SAID NO TO DRUGS AND ALCHOL
REPUBLIC ** PICTURES

This is _____ *to Certify that*

_____

Has said No to Drugs and Alcohol
Sunset Carson, Republic Pictures Corp.
. . . 12636 Beatrice St. P.O.Box. 66930 . . .
Los Angeles, Ca. 90068-6930

(Sunset continues) My dad worked in rodeos. I started out in rodeo, and Tom Mix saw me and offered me a job. I did some trick riding, and I loaded Tom's guns for his shooting act. Later on, I did the shooting acts just like the ones Tom did.

My name was Mickey Harrison (not true), but Republic didn't like the name. They came up with the name Carson for my last name. Then they kicked around several combinations like "Cody" Carson and others. Well, old man Yates looked out the window and saw a used car lot with a sign that read "Sunset

Motors." He said, "That's it — Sunset Carson!" He named me after that used car lot. I'm sure glad he didn't name me "Motors Carson."

I received second billing behind Smiley Burnette in our four pictures because he was smaller than me (Laugh). You couldn't see a 165 pound, 17-year-old kid (obviously Carson was lying about his age, since he was born in 1920), whipping a 289-pound man, so I didn't give him no argument. Smiley was kinda cold for our first couple of films and, as a newcomer, you could get pretty nervous working with a guy who'd been in those Westerns a long time. I don't know if he was told to or not, but he kinda softened up around the last picture. But Smiley was a great guy to work with. The only thing we had to watch was his milk shakes and ice cream. I never saw anyone eat so much ice cream. He was always eating (Laugh).

Smiley didn't own his horse, Ringeye, the one he rode all the time in the movies. It belonged to the studio, and the ring around its eye was painted on with one of those little brushes that came in those small bottles of shoe polish. Smiley rode all over the horse, but he stayed on.

They had originally intended for me to do more pictures with Smiley but, after a while, the fan mail was coming in pretty good for me, and they decided to let me go on my own.

I would have loved to have had Gabby Hayes in my pictures. He was not only funny, he was a fine actor who could make you cry. Gabby was the measuring stick with which to judge all sidekicks. He was always a gentleman ... and a sharp dresser.

I had a difficult time starting off. It was hard to remember your lines and concentrate on where you had to be during filming. And it was long and hard work — sometimes from 5:00 in the morning until midnight. We'd go up to Iverson's Ranch, which was about 50 miles away, and shoot the riding scenes. Then we would go back to the studio to shoot some more. When it rained, we would shoot the inside scenes. They wasted no time. When the pictures were completed, we would go on tour to theaters where they were being shown. Most of the cowboys did this; we picked up a little extra income that way

Harry Woods was the heavy in my first picture. At the time, I was about 160 or 170 pounds. Old Harry was about 6-3 and weighed about 250. He asked me if I knew how to picture fight and, of course, I told him I did. Hell, I didn't! I'm supposed to grab him, whirl him around and knock him in the water trough. I had my back to the trough, and threw a punch. I'm supposed to catch him, whirl him around and throw him in it. When they yelled "Action!", he comes across and hits me right on the button. I hit the water trough, and it was about an hour before I was able to work again. Old "Pappy" Yates came down and said. "So you know how to fight, cowboy? Every time you are not in a scene in this picture, I want you and some of the stunt-men to go out back and practice." So I went out there with guys like Tom Steele and Dale Van Sickel, and they taught me how to screen fight.

I hit a guy one time, too. I can't remember his name, but he told them he could do stunt fights. He was doubled in some of the fighting, but they had to put him in for a close-up. Right before the scene, he said, "Sunset, I don't know how to do a movie fight, and I'm scared to death." I said, 'Well, you swing across like you're hitting my shoulder, and I'll block it and swing across your chin and hit your shoulder and knock you out of the scene. You snap your head back like I had hit you on the chin.' Well, just as I swung, he dropped his head towards the shoulder I was going to hit. I hit him right on the button, and he went down. When the director hollered, 'Cut!', two of the propmen grabbed the guy and dragged him out. They took him out back and gave him some water and straightened him out. Those guys stick together, and they knew he would be in trouble with the director, so they covered for him. The director didn't know a danged thing about it until the picture was over.

One time, we worked until about midnight, but we still had to be at the studio the next morning at 5:00. I got up and took a cold shower to help wake me up. It didn't help much. After shaving, I thought I was putting on shaving lotion, but I rubbed my face all over with Absorbine Jr. (a liniment). My face was so red they didn't have to put any make-up on me.

It was the director who came up with the idea of me winking and making a tongue-clicking sound at Linda Stirling in SHERIFF OF CIMARRON (1945). It was a little thing, but it brought in a lot of mail. I broke my arm in that picture. If you notice in the fight scene, I came up slow. We had only a couple of close-up scenes, and one walking across the street, and the film would be finished. When I'm walking across the street, you'll notice I have my hand on my gun. I can notice about there where my arm is broken and where it shows up doing dialogue. I was lucky it happened on the last day of shooting — about 11:00 in the morning.

We worked until about midnight, and I didn't tell Yak (Yakima Canutt got full credit for directing the picture) that it was broken until one of the last scenes. It's in the scene where I said, "Tex, you framed me." If you look real close, you'll see pain etched across my face. Yak said that we'd have to wrap it up. You'll notice that when I'm walking across the street, my hand is on my gun, but when I come through the door my arm is swinging. That's because we did the first and last scene on the first day of shooting. When I catch Linda Stirling falling off the ladder while adjusting the clock, I'd go around back and change shirts and then come back, walk through the door with the other shirt and catch her in my arms. If we hadn't done it that way I could never have caught her with my broken arm.

(Note: Canutt confirmed Sunset's story: "We worked all day on a Sunset Carson picture. Late in the day, I looked at Sunset, and he had tears in his eyes. I discovered he had been working since morning with a broken arm.")

A bunch of us Republic cowboys were in the Roy Rogers picture BELLS OF ROSARITA (1945). They brought in me,

Bill Elliott, Bob Livingston, Allan Lane and Don Barry for small roles in the picture. In the scene where we're shooting at the outlaws, Bob turned to Rocky and ad-libbed, "You're going to do a lot of damage with those blanks." And they left it in the picture (Laugh). I guess I worked four or five days over a period of a couple of weeks. Then, after using us, they cut out a lot of what we did. It turned out to be a real good picture. I was told later Bill Elliott got $2,000 for his part. If he did, that's sure a whole lot more than the rest of us got.

(Note: According to Jack Mathis' excellent book, Republic Confidential, Volume 2, The Players, *Elliott did, indeed, get paid $2,000 for his cameo appearance in the film. He also waived the top-billing clause in his contract, providing he was credited first of the other cowboy guest stars. There was also a provision in Elliott's contract, when he signed with Republic, that he did not have to do serials. While at Republic, Sunset was a under a term contract which guaranteed him 40 weeks of employment. The salary was $150 per week for the first year, escalating to $200/week for the second and $250/week for year three. The contract was in effect from March 18, 1944, through July 15, 1946. Sunset called his horse Silver in the BELLS OF ROSARITA. It was the same animal that had been ridden in the two Lone Ranger serials. Robert Livingston, who had ridden the horse in the 1939 serial, THE LONE RANGER RIDES AGAIN, also rode it in the last four of his* Three Mesquiteers *films and in his last three starring pictures at Republic. The same horse was also ridden by Tom Tyler in his* Three Mesquiteers *series.)*

(Sunset talks about his horse): He could really run. If you notice when I was riding with the other cowboys in BELLS OF ROSARITA, I had to hold him back some. At first, I called the horse Silver, but the Lone Ranger was real popular at the time, so I changed the name to Cactus. He was sired by Buck Jones' Silver and, if Buck had not have been killed in that fire, he was going to use the horse in his next pictures. I bought the horse from Buck Jones' widow. If you'll notice, I always rode with one hand on my movies. I got used to riding with one hand when I was working in rodeos.

(Note: The statements about the horse being sired by Buck Jones' Silver, and buying the animal from Mrs. Jones cannot be confirmed, and are probably not true. Apparently, the horse was rented by Republic. There is no record of any screen appearances by the horse after Sunset's Republic series ended in 1946.)

(Merrill McCord, in his wonderfully researched book, *Brothers of the West: The Lives and Films of Robert Livingston and Jack Randall,* confirmed that Sunset's horse was the same animal that had been ridden by Lee Powell and Robert Livingston in the Lone Ranger serials.)

The movies I made after leaving Republic weren't worth a dime. They made them in color, but cheap. I had to do my own stunts and everything. I went on tour with the pictures. Maybe some were released in black and white, but the ones I went with were in color. We were sold a bill of goods on those films, me and my manager. They were supposed to be up to certain standards and they weren't. I was into the trap before I knew what happened. They told us what the budget was supposed to be, and we'd get out there and find something different.

(Note: The films may have been shot in 16mm color and blown up to 35mm for theatrical distribution. In the process, the color was probably so grainy that most of the films saw only sporadic black and white release. It is certain that SUNSET CARSON RIDES AGAIN (Yucca, 1947) was filmed in color.)

Dale, my brother, came out to do a few of these movies with me. One day, he was riding the lead horse with the bandits, and they were really carrying the mail (running full speed). His horse stepped into a hole or something and went down, and 20 horses went over him. I was sitting behind the camera praying; I just knew he had been killed. But when the smoke and dust cleared, he got up and rubbed the dirt out of his eyes and said: "Will someone catch that danged horse for me?"

Sunset with his brother Herman Dale Harrison.

My picture, RIO GRANDE (a miserable film — not to be confused with the excellent John Wayne movie), was produced by a Texas outfit. It was filmed about 25 miles east of Laredo, in Juanita, Texas. It was an actual Spanish town that they claimed Pancho Villa had built for his girl friend. We filmed a lot of it at night, and the moths were so thick that every time I said lines, I was afraid I would swallow one. You can even see moths in the picture.

Some years later, I was I was almost killed by a hit-and-run driver. It happened one night about 11:00 when I decided to go across the street from my motel to get something to eat. I waited for the light to change and started across the street; I heard the car coming and threw up my arms across my chest. The car hit me and ran over my arm. Some people picked me up and took me to the hospital. My heart was bruised, my chest swollen, one lung was full of liquid, my arm completely crushed, and my shoulder was powdered. When they cut me open, they found a hole in my liver. After they put me back together, I had double pneumonia.

Lash LaRue came to visit me in the hospital. I don't know how he got into the operating room. *(Note: It was probably because, at one time, LaRue was professing to be a preacher.)*

I recognized his voice, but I wasn't sure I wasn't hearing things. He came in clean-cut and he looked terrific. He said, "The Lord's brought you back for something. It's not your time to go. He's got something lined out for you to do on this earth." He took his Bible, said a prayer, and then he left. He came back about three days later with a box of fruit, and some pictures for the nurses. Lash is a good old boy, but he is the only cowboy to star in an X-rated movie. I never saw it, but it's called, wouldn't you know, HARD ON THE TRAIL.

The children of today are looking for heroes like the B-Western cowboys. They need to see clean movies where good always overcomes evil. I know had my heroes as a kid. I liked Tom Mix, Ken Maynard, Buck Jones, and Hoot Gibson — the old Hooter. I'm proud to say that I met all of them. The 50,000 letters we received after the first run of "Six Gun Heroes" shows there's a lot of interest in the old B-Westerns.

I would have liked to have made it in the big Westerns but, if you think about it, you will see that some of the guys who made it in the big ones were 45 to 50 years old before they made that kind of Western. Look at Randolph Scott. Look at Duke (John Wayne); he was 50 before he was ripe enough to know what the heck he was doing and how to do it. You finally learn.

Everybody wanted my type of Western to come back. So I got some boys together and produced MARSHAL OF WINDY HOLLOW up in Kentucky. I did my own stunts, and we brought in Ken Maynard and some of the boys from the coast. We had 35 covered wagons, mules, beautiful location, a Western town, and we made a heck of a good Western. But we had a wise guy who stole the negative; it was like cattle rustling. This was the first time I ever heard of someone stealing a negative. We had lawsuits trying to get it back, but he hid it someplace. He bought out some of the stockholders, but I'll see it rot in hell before I'll sign a release because I put my blood into it.

(Earlier Sunset had said of the movie: "If it clicks, like I'm

positive it will, I'll be making a whole string of Westerns again — just like I used to.)

(See the section on The Making of Marshal of Windy Hollow.)

Sunset visits with young fan Doneen Key (right) and her cousin Neil. Since meeting Sunset Carson in 1986, Doneen has been a regular film festival attendee for the past 20 years. Sunset took a special interest in Doneen, sending her gifts and cards for special occasions until his death. Other celebrities Doneen has stayed in touch with include Donna Martell, Neil Summers, Donna Douglas, and Ruth Reinhart.

SUNSET TALKS ABOUT HIS PALS

I met Buck Jones at a rodeo in San Francisco. We got pretty well acquainted. Later, I went on the set where Buck was making a movie. They had brought in a prizefighter to do a fight scene with Buck. The prizefighter told them he knew how to movie fight. Well, on the first shot, he hit Buck right on the chin and turned him a flip. Buck went over and put his head in a bucket of water and came back. Bam! The prizefighter hit Buck again. Buck went back and put his head in the bucket, and they doctored him up a bit. They started the fight again, and for the third time the prizefighter knocks Buck down. Buck puts his head back into the water, and goes over to the camera man and says, "Keep the damn thing rolling." The prizefighter didn't get a chance to hit Buck again; Buck waded into him and beat that guy into the ground — and that guy was a prizefighter! Buck was plenty tough.

Nellie Walker was one of Hollywood's best stunt riders. I won't tell you who it was, but she doubled one of Republic's cowboy stars (due to his size, it may have been Don Barry; however, Barry's main stunter was Bill Yrigoyen whose more famous brother Joe doubled Gene Autry, Roy Rogers, and Rex Allen.)

(While he was in Hollywood, stuntwoman Nellie Walker was president of the Sunset Carson Fan Club.)

"SUNSET" CARSON FAN CLUB

Join the "Sunset" Carson Fan Club. Members receive membership card, personally autographed photo of "Sunset," the "Sunset" Journal every three months, plus snapshots of every conceivable Western Star—on the average of eight in each and every issue of the Journal, including two stories of "Sunset's" latest pictures and photos.

If you are interested in the West and any thing and every thing pertaining to the West, this is the club for you! Membership dues $1.00 per year.

Send dues to club President—

Nellie Walker
Box 3128
Hollywood, California

I had the pleasure of working with Tom London. I killed him a few times and then he turned out to be my comedian. He was a terrific, terrific comedian and a wonderful person to work with. He didn't wear his teeth when he was my sidekick. There were a couple of times when we took lunch breaks, and Tom would put his teeth back in to eat. Then we'd go back to filming and after a couple of takes, the director would holler, "Cut!" And then say, "Gosh, Tom, you forget to take your teeth out." We had to reshoot those scenes.

Yakima Canutt is the best stuntman that ever lived. He set the trend for the other stuntmen who followed. I was pleased to have Yak direct my picture, SHERIFF OF CIMARRON (Republic, 1945). He was easy to get along with and he knew his business. When they needed a good action scene, they called Yak in.

Black Jack O' Shea (real name John Rellaford) was a badman in a bunch of my movies, but we didn't mix it up very much. Jack was a little guy, and it wouldn't look right for me to be whipping up on him.

We had this scene where I had to carry Monte Hale from the stagecoach inside to a table. When we got inside, Tommy Carr (director) said: "Monte, a dead man doesn't smile." So we go back out for the second time, and I'm carrying Monte back in, and he bursts out laughing. Tommy Carr said: "Okay, we're going to break for lunch and when we come back, we're going to do it one more time and that's it." So when we came back, Monte said: "Sunset you look in one direction, and I'll look in the other, and maybe we can get this thing done." We got it done, and I carried Monte okay, but it was hard trying to go up the steps with the big guy while looking in another direction.

One day I was on the set with Monte and Roy Barcroft (real name Howard Ravenscroft). We were having lunch when Monte pulled out his pistol and said. "Don't move Roy, there is a snake crawling out from the rock where you're sitting." Old Roy just grinned and said: "Don't shoot it Monte: it may be someone from the front office."

Barcroft was one of my best friends. He would play tricks on all the actors. He really enjoyed being one of the meanest guys on the screen, but he was one of the nicest guys in the world; he was a real cream puff. Me and Peggy and Linda really loved the guy.

Charlie King and I were on tour in some small town in Oklahoma. One morning we stopped for breakfast at this little restaurant. I think the waitress recognized us because she brought my breakfast and set it down gently with a smile. She practically threw the plate at Charlie. She slammed it down in front of him as if he was a mad dog or something. Old Charlie never said a word. He just looked over at me and winked, but he left her a nice tip. After we ate, we were headed back to the car when some kids came walking down the road. They were about 10 or 11 years old. They looked us over and one said: "Yeah, it's Sunset Carson!" The other one said: "And that's that mean old back-shooting S.O.B. Let's get him!" They picked up some rocks and started throwing them at old Charlie. He had to run to the car for cover.

I never worked with Pat Buttram, but he is one of the funniest guys I ever met. He can come up with funny things right off the top off his head. I always enjoy the show when Pat's part of it. He's a real pal to Gene Autry. You would never expect a cowboy to own a baseball team, but Gene does. Old Pat said: "Gene used to ride off in the sunset, but now he owns it" (Laugh).

I always admired Ken Maynard as a rider. I never once considered myself better than Ken — but nearly as good.

I stopped by to see Clayton Moore when he was making a personal appearance in Kentucky. When Clayton wanted a cigarette, he would go to where the kids couldn't see him smoke. He knew they would be disappointed to see the Lone Ranger smoking a cigarette. I liked that about Clayton.

Tim McCoy was such a proper gentleman. He had been a Colonel in the Army. I remember his movies when he would come in and roll his eyes side to side. Those mean eyes of his made some of the kids, on the front row, move back several rows. Tim was working for Tommy Scott's Wild West Show when he had to get a pacemaker put in. They called me to replace him, and I completed the tour. Tim came back, but when he got sick again, I was called back. This time Tim retired.

Old Earle Hodgins was quite a character; he was a regular around the studio. He didn't follow the script. He would just take off and do his thing and then turn it over to someone else. Earle drank a lot. One day he came in with a brown bag that went "clank, clank." They asked him what he had in the bag, and he said "It's my lunch." Of course, everyone knew what was in the bag. He would come in drinking and with real dark glasses on, and he would take them off and look up to see if the sun was shining.

Snake oil salesman Earle Hodgins.

THEY KNEW SUNSET

Betty Burbridge (screenwriter): Sunset was a dear boy, but he liked nothing better than to come into my office, sit down in a chair with his feet on my desk, kick the other chair back and tell me what a great star he was, and how I should write his next script. Suggestions I never minded, but Sunset just didn't realize that regardless of how I wrote the scripts, the pictures would turn out with the same odor. The few people who tried to tell him what was wrong with his pictures finally gave up trying, as it seemed to go in one ear and out the other.

Lesley Selander (director): I first time I set eyes on Sunset Carson, he was completely decked out in a cowboy outfit with a hand-tooled gun belt, but he didn't know how to ride a horse. After a time, he became an excellent rider, but out of the saddle he was as clumsy as ever. Acting wasn't his thing. But he was a good-looking kid, and we figured the only way he could overcome his shortcomings as an actor was action, action, and more action.

(Note: Could Selander's memory have failed him? His comment about Sunset's lack of rider ability is startling since everyone else stated he was an excellent horseman.)

Thomas Carr (director): Sunset was a great big kid … something like 6-7, boots added three inches to him, and you're up to 6-10. You add a ten-gallon hat, you're up to seven feet — and the doorway was only 6-8. So, anytime he made a fast exit, he had to duck before he went through a door, or he'd lose his hat. We had to make the doors and ceilings a little higher, but we didn't take into consideration if he had to go in a hurry. He wasn't quite sure which direction he was going to go. He'd head for a door and sometimes hit his right shoulder or left side on the door and take half the door out. You never knew exactly what was going to happen with Sunset. But he learned like they all do. Sunset was an awfully sweet guy and he tried as hard as he could and eventually worked into a pretty good Western star. He was much like Whip Wilson.

I would never have chosen to work with Sunset, as there was not much you could do with him. He was no actor, and as a Western star he made a good rodeo performer — which is where he came from. Some of those rodeo people were pretty rough, two-fisted drinkers. Sunset was known to take a drink and sometimes showed up on the set loaded. I got mad and threatened to bend a piece of 2x4 lumber over his head if he ever got drunk again on one of my pictures. We got along after that, but I still can't believe how I got away with it — he was about a foot taller than I was! The first film we did together was SANTA FE SADDLEMATES (Republic, 1945); it was this film that labeled me as an action director. I never saw myself as that, but the way people enthuse at conventions you'd think it should have been awarded an Oscar.

Peggy Stewart (real name Margaret O'Rourke): He was like a bull in a China shop. For a man that had rodeoed, I never saw anybody so accident prone in all my whole put together. He was tall, and he was awkward.

In CODE OF THE PRAIRIE (Republic, 1944), Tom Chatterton was playing Bat Matson. We kept telling Sunset before the scene it's Matt Bastardson. Sunset would parrot whatever he heard us say. We did about six takes on this — Sunset goes in and says, "Matt Bastardson." Director Spencer Bennet became really impatient because jeepers, to do six takes on a Western was absolutely unheard of — you don't do that! Get it in two or forget it and move on to the next scene. So, I told him, "Really, it is Bat Matson." This time Sunset got it right — you can see Spence go, "Whew, we got passed that." Sunset says, "Yeah, he's up in the hills chasing them smurfugglers." You gotta love him. I used to kid Sunset, "Uh-huh, I know you asked for Linda Stirling (to be in his pictures) instead of me."

Kirk "Superman" Alyn (real name John Feggo Jr.): I had worked in New York doing plays and radio. I was getting so little sleep doing both that I decided to quit and take a vacation to California. Well, I was there for a while and decided, since I was there, I might as will try to get some picture work. I got an agent, and the first place he took me was to Republic. It was on a Bill Elliott picture. The man originally scheduled to play the part had to have an emergency appendectomy. The director said I looked a lot like the man and could even wear his clothes. That was my first picture, and my second picture was with Sunset. I admired the way he rode and the way he handled the bullwhip. In the picture, I stole his horse.

Linda Stirling (real name Louise Schultz): Sunset never took anything too seriously. You were very comfortable around him. My favorite picture has got to be SANTA FE SADDLEMATES (Republic, 1945) with Sunset Carson. I got to play a real part instead of just being the girl at the door waving the guy off into the sunset, no pun intended. Generally, we stood around and wrung our hands, and they told us what they were about to do and we would end up saying, "Bye." But in this one I got to wear a very sexy dress in the saloon while I was pretending to be a saloon singer … the plot is very complicated. It was a fun picture, and I loved it.

Unlike Sunset, I had no skill whatsoever with horses and,

more than once, the crew would find me sprawled in the dust or crumpled in the bushes somewhere after my horse had run away with me. I must have fallen off every horse I was ever on. I just went up one side and down on the other. My horsemanship left a great deal to be desired. I remember once Spencer Bennet (director) asked me if I could do a running insert I said sure, although I had no idea what it was. To my dismay, I found out. My horse took it as a personal challenge to outrun the camera truck, and I went along for the ride, taking in scenery from side to side and end to end on the galloping beast. Horses and I never really got on a first-name basis or shared social lives.

(Note: To film a running insert, a camera car moves ahead of a running horse and rider.)

Pierce Lyden: I worked with Sunset a few times. He was a good cowboy and one of the best riders of all the stars with whom I worked.

Tom London (real name Leonard Clapham): You've heard the expression "as green as a gourd." Well that was Sunset as an actor. I tried to help him all I could, and he tried hard.

Monte Hale: In one picture, we were doing a running and shooting scene, and I was right behind Sunset. I powder burned him right behind his ears. I had just been to the dentist a couple of days before to get a three-tooth bridge put in. After the ride, I hurried up to apologize to Sunset, and my bridge popped out, and a horse stepped on it and broke it. I told Sunset that if he ever told any of the crew about it that I would kill him (Laugh).

Tim McCoy: I'd never met Sunset until he came to take my place with Tommy Scott when I got sick. You see I was thrown into the hospital with this bad back. I couldn't walk. It was a slipped disc. So I said, "The hell with it. This is it. I'm going to quit. I'm going home. I've had enough punishment." And Tommy said, "What about next season?" And I said, "No, I've done my last season," so he brought in Sunset.

June Carr (Discussing her road show): Sunset Carson was a big Western star. We met him through Spade Cooley. The women went crazy over him. When the show was over, we had to hide him (from the women). He was just gorgeous. We got him on a contract and took him out. I didn't go because no woman could ever handle Sunset. Ron (Ormond) worked with him on the show. For 13 weeks, Sunset Carson never saw a sober day. He was drunk all the time, very hard to work with.

(Note: Carr was also an actress, and she was married to Ron Ormond who was associated with the final 12 Lash LaRue B-Western movies at Western Adventure Productions that were released from 1948 through 1952.)

Tommy Scott: Sunset was a nice fellow. He worked off and on for me a few years. On one of our tours in Canada, we had a string of vehicles, and Sunset was in a very small trailer being pulled by one of the cars in the rear. We came to a little town that had one red light and it caught us. Sunset was back in that trailer with only his bathing suit on. He had quite a bit of money on him — he must have had it stuck in his bathing suit. Well, when we had to stop for that red light, I guess Sunset saw a Budweiser sign somewhere and got out of the trailer to buy a beer. When the light changed, we went on. We traveled several miles down the road before we stopped for a break. Sunset's wife went back to the trailer and discovered Sunset missing. She asked everyone if he was with them, but he was not to be found. Before too long, here came a cab with Sunset — still in his bathing suit, and with no money. He had to get money from his wife to pay the cab fare. I guess he spent all the money buying drinks for the guys back there at the beer joint, but that was just like Sunset. I never had a problem with Sunset drinking on the job.

(Note: Scott operated a Wild West Show for many years. Sunset worked for him for a little over three years. Others who worked with Scott included Tim McCoy, Johnny Mack Brown, and Fuzzy St. John.)

Sunset with Tommy Scott and Tim McCoy.

THE FANS SPEAK

(I have asked some of the most knowledgeable Western film fans to give their views on Sunset. When I asked them to contribute their thoughts, I knew there would be repetition. For this, I apologize, but I did not think it right to edit their comments.)

Dale Berry (entertainer): I toured for awhile with and, at times, he stayed at my house here in Dallas and at my place in Los Angeles. I remember we made a personal appearance at a black theatre down South — I think it was on the Bijou Theatre circuit — somewhere in Mississippi. After the movie was shown, I came on stage with my guitar, sung a couple of songs, and cracked some corny jokes. And just as we had done in our other appearances, I introduced Sunset and asked for big round of applause. After much clapping, and everyone looking around — there was no Sunset. I apologized to the audience and said, "Well, let's try it one more time." I introduced Sunset and said, "Here he is, Republic's action ace and everyone's favorite cowboy star, Sunset Carson. Let's give him a big welcome." Then Sunset came down the center aisle of the theatre and fired a couple of fully loaded five-in-one blanks, which sounded like a cannon explosion. In about 10 to 15 seconds, the place was empty with no one but Sunset, the manager, and me left in the theatre. We could see scared eyes peeping around the corners. It was only after I reassured the kids that Sunset was shooting blanks that they got up enough courage to return to their seats.

This incident caused me to suggest to Sunset that we should change our opening act for the rest of the tour, and we did. From then on, after my introduction, Sunset would just walk in from the side of the stage. He talked about making his movies, answered questions, and then ran a short film clip of himself riding, fighting, etc. After Sunset's part of the show, I would return to the stage, sing another song, and tell the fans we would be in the lobby signing autographs.

In California, I had a place up in the Outpost, which was a very exclusive section of old Hollywood. Sunset would often bunk in with me. He had an old F-hole guitar. I had no idea that he could play or sing. But he got it out and played and sang a couple of songs, and he was really very good. Sunset gave me money to go pick up some fried chicken and by the time I got back, he had put away his guitar, and I never heard him sing again. Lash LaRue sang for me one night, too, and he was just great. I never knew Lash could sing either.

Sunset had bought an expensive video camera, and we, along with some other actors, filmed a couple of days at a Western street. I may have some of that old footage around the house. Wouldn't it be neat to see some of the last footage shot of Sunset?

(Note: Actress Barbra Fuller, one of Lash's 12 wives, told of her and Lash often going to a nightclub (or restaurant) where Lash would sometimes sing. She said he had a very good voice, and could sing as well as any of the movie singing cowboys.)

Les Adams (author): I saw Sunset's first Western on original release when I was 10, and saw the rest of the Republics as they were released. At the time, I thought he was the best Western film hero I had seen ... except when he talked. I was just a kid, but I knew he was way short of acting skills, and I didn't even know that such existed. I just knew there was something bothersome when it came to Sunset Carson and dialogue. But he more than made up for that, both in appearance and action. Plus, Republic gave him good support in the casts and plots.

Sunset, who it appears was his own worst enemy, could have and should have been at the top of the Western-cowboys list for at least 10 years. And, watching his films now, I no longer think he was the worst at dialogue that ever came along ... I've seen all of the Reb Russell pictures now.

I rate all of the Sunset Carsons at Republic about even (after Smiley left), but the one I like least is the one that had Bob Steele as his brother. They could have, at least, made one of them adopted.

Jim Martin (member of the Gun-Spinning Hall of Fame): I was living in Huntington Park, California, during the war; this would have been around 1944 or '45. I went to the old Lyric Theater there, and Sunset was doing a personal appearance in conjunction with a couple of his movies. He was doing some gun tricks and a few rope tricks on the stage, and asked if anyone would like to come on the stage to see the tricks up close. I was one of the kids that made a beeline up to the stage. He shook my hand, and I remember that he was probably the tallest guy I had ever met in my young life.

Jim Hamby (a fan): In 1980, at the Charlotte, North Carolina, Western Film Fair, on a Saturday night after the banquet, Sunset was in the hotel bar and was intoxicated to the point that he could hardly walk. He was accompanied by a local disc-jockey called "Slick" who was about 5-7 and 150 pounds. Slick made every attempt to carry the 6-6 cowboy out of the bar at closing time. Of course, it was an impossible task for the small guy, so he enlisted the aid of three larger men and successfully managed to get Sunset to his room. Naturally, this was disappointing to the fans, and I'm sure it was to Sunset once he sobered up.

Ross Pittman (a fan): Back in the late 1940s, several of the B-Western stars would make appearances at various little theaters around the country including Tex Ritter and his horse White Flash, Rocky Lane, Lash LaRue, Dub Taylor, Sunset, and a few others. Anyway, Sunset and a small group of musicians were to appear at one of the local theaters in Columbia, Mississippi (my hometown), where they were scheduled to put on two shows, one 4:00 in the afternoon and another at 8:00 that night.

I don't remember the feature film, but it was one of Sunset's Westerns. Well, 4:00 o'clock game around and no Sunset, 5:00 o'clock and no Sunset, around 7:00 or a little after, Sunset and the group came driving up … well "juiced." The owner of the theater, by this time, was highly perturbed because they had shown the Western several times, even added a feature, but a lot of the people had gone home. Those who were still there were greatly upset, so the owner was going to refund everybody's money, and told Sunset he could get on down the road. Sunset, being as tall as he was, and the owner of the theater (about 5-9) inches tall confronted each other, and Sunset told him, "Hell no, I came to put on a show, and I am going to put on a show."

All went well for the few of us who were left. Sunset did the regular routine, quick draw, etc. and the band played and sang a few songs. Afterwards, Sunset signed a few autographs but, during the show, someone tore a hole in the screen and that set off another problem. I never knew how it came out, but all in all it was a good show, well worth the wait.

Hans Wollstein (author): I'm actually quite a fan of Sunset Carson. He looked like a cowboy, he spoke like a cowboy, and he rode like a cowboy. He may not have been the greatest thespian around, and some have compared his acting ability to the earlier Reb Russell who is supposedly the worst actor among the Hollywood cowboys. But unlike Reb, who was mired in independent low-budget oaters, Sunset was given the best Republic had to offer: good stories, the studio's famous technical know-how, and great supporting casts. His later Westerns for Oliver Drake and Yucca Pictures are utterly miserable, but Drake was forced to film "faster and furiouser" (to borrow from Sam Z. Arkoff) than almost anybody else, and not even a William Boyd or a Buck Jones would have stood a chance under his supervision. Like so many others, I re-discovered Sunset when, late in life, he hosted a series of B-Western retrospectives broadcast on PBS. In fact, my devotion to the genre stems from watching Sunset introduce the likes of Bob Steele and the young John Wayne on the local CUNY station in New York. He still hadn't learned to act — or even read cue cards — but there was something wonderfully authentic about the guy, and he will be missed.

Paul Dellinger (author): Sunset made some great Westerns at Republic, some of which I like to watch repeatedly. I've seen some he made afterward and feel those are best forgotten (although he wasn't bad in his brief role, along with Don Barry, in BUCKSTONE COUNTY PRISON for independent North Carolina producer/actor Earl Owensby). He wasn't a great actor, but delivered the action. I enjoyed all his Republic movies, despite his never having a regular comic sidekick, and alternating between wearing one and two guns which somehow puzzled me as a kid. He didn't have the continuity some of the other actors had in their series. (The four early movies he made with Smiley were good, but not as good as what followed at Republic — except for FIREBRANDS OF ARIZONA (1944) which was a great comedy.)

I did like Sunset (in the Republics). When I watched his movies as a kid, he often seemed much like a kid himself, a bigger and tougher version of what we wanted to be. He had good support, mostly good scripts, good leading ladies and outstanding action. Sometimes, the action moved almost too fast, as in SANTA FE SADDLEMATES (Republic, 1945) where it goes so fast that leading lady Linda Stirling never even has a chance to give her character's name.

Sunset always played Sunset, and always pretty much the same way. If I had to pick a favorite, I probably couldn't narrow it down to fewer than three: SHERIFF OF CIMARRON, SANTA FE SADDLEMATES, and ROUGH RIDERS OF CHEYENNE, all 1945.

Clint Mitchell (a fan): I was at an age when everything was magic and I believed all I saw on the movie screen. If the cowboy was fighting a crook and he was on top of a mountain — I thought he was on top of the mountain. It never occurred to me that might just be on a rock with net close by to catch the loser, who was almost always the crook. So when I saw Sunset Carson, I believed he was a real-life hero. It's easy for someone to say, "He looked every inch the cowboy. That is, until he stepped off his horse and said his lines."

Maybe as an adult and many years later, we can discredit him, but he was there on the screen doing his best, and we were just kids watching our hero fight the baddies. Just ask yourself, "Would it have been better had he not been on the scene?" I don't think so. He looked great to me, and he'll always be the kind of hero I would have wanted to be. If I would say anything to discredit Sunset, I would feel as if I had joined the crooks fighting against him. So when I'm asked, did Sunset make a positive contribution to Western films, I answer with a resounding "YES!"

Jim Kocher (a fan): While he was not the world's greatest actor, he was one of the best action players in the B-Westerns. It must have been his training on the rodeo circuit that made him such a good horseman. He was an outstanding action actor. No singing, just action. His fight scenes were very realistic especially to 8-10 year old boys, and those were the ones that the old cowboy movies appealed to mostly.

Bill Russell (author): Sunset came along a little bit too late to really my garner attention. Also, by that time I did not see him on the screen since I had "growed up" more or less and didn't go to the Saturday matinees any longer. However, I've seen a many of his films in past years. I personally think SANTA FE SADDLEMATES (1945) was his best, with SHERIFF OF CIMARRON (1945) a close second. If he could have delivered his lines better (or remembered them) and had come along a little earlier, I believe he would have been one of Republic's all-time top stars. But the action aspect of his pictures was loaded. I always thought he would have made a helluva silent cowboy star.

Boyd Magers (Western film historian and publisher): 6-6 Sunset Carson had the B-Western world by the tail and blew it through his own inexperience and problems with "who kicked John." The young, slow-drawl, Texas rodeo rider came to Republic in 1944 — second billed to Smiley Burnette at first. No other sidekick ever achieved top billing over the leading man, but Smiley was hot (and demanding) at Republic following his days with Gene Autry. With Autry away in the service and the failure of Eddie Dew's *John Paul Revere* series in which Smiley had co-starred, Republic acquiesced to Smiley's starring demands and started out "Sonny" Carson second billed to Smiley.

After only four films, Smiley was headed to Columbia as Sunset's fan mail was pouring in. (At one time it's said Carson's fan mail rivaled that of Roy Rogers!) In Sunset's solo films, action, action and more action was the byword. Incidentally, note that Sunset uses a bullwhip to snatch an outlaw off his horse years before it ever occurred to Lash LaRue or Whip Wilson. Sadly, booze got the better of Sunset. Apparently,

Republic President Herbert J. Yates had warned Sunset about the bottle and eventually, true to his word, let Sunset go at the height of his popularity after only 15 films.

When I compiled a TOP 100 COWBOYS OF THE CENTURY special edition of *Western Clippings*, I ranked Sunset at #32. Had Sunset made more at Republic, where would his standing in the Top 100 be today—no doubt much higher as the good ol' boy seemed to have what action-minded moviegoers wanted. Trying for a comeback, but still battling booze, the no-budget Astor films he made (although in color — their one redeeming factor) in 1947 were a sad codicil to his Republic titles.

Sunset toured the world for years from England to Siam. In his later years, he enjoyed new-found fame as one of the most popular guest stars on the Western film festival trail. The fans remembered him fondly.

My personal favorites of Sunset's Westerns are SANTA FE SADDLEMATES (1945) and THE CHEROKEE FLASH (1945) with RED RIVER RENEGADES (1946) a hot third. In SANTA FE SADDLEMATES, Sunset's in top form; he never looked fitter. THE CHEROKEE FLASH is one of Republic's most unusual Westerns, in that it gives heavy Roy Barcroft a sympathetic role as Sunset's foster father.

Grady Franklin (former publisher of *The Western Film*): He sure was a handsome dude. Tall, good looking, great riding a horse. The lassies just had to love him back in the middle 1940s when he came blazing across the silver screen at Republic Pictures.

Sunset Carson. What a name for a cowboy star. And he was a star. Maybe he didn't sound like a star when he attempted to deliver his lines, but he had star power in the arenas (no pun intended) in which he participated.

"Howdy Pardners, I'm Sunset Carson." He said those words

in his later years with the same slow drawl of the Southwest that marked his screen appearances from 1944 and into the 1950s. That familiar phrase was from the "Six Gun Heroes" television series in the 1980s. He introduced the films in that PBS program, and rode like the wind in some of the selected shoot-em-ups viewed nationwide.

While the peak of his career came in the 1940s, Sunset made new friends and new fans throughout the 1980s when he attended the Western film conventions. He was a fixture especially at the Western Film Fair in Charlotte, North Carolina, showing up oftentimes as a fan rather than an invited guest star with full expenses paid by the organizing committee. His lanky frame was a welcome sight and in later appearances he seemed to suffer from various ailments and injuries.

In between his glory days at Republic and the film festivals, Sunset was in a few films which were less than great. One of them, filmed in Kentucky rather than in the Wild West, apparently has disappeared altogether. Or at least from the silver screen.

I never met Sunset until we came face to face in the 1980s at Charlotte, Knoxville, Memphis and Portsmouth. This period, from 1979 into the 1990s, was a time when I was active as a writer-photographer at the festivals.

He was as impressive in person as he was on the screen. Age did not diminish his handsome features. And, as most often is the case with people from the South and Southwest, he kept the laid back personality of a slow talking and slow moving gentleman. You know, like Johnny Mack Brown of Alabama or Sammy Baugh of Texas. You couldn't help but like Sunset. He was easy to talk to and easy to listen to. However, there were times when one wished for him to speak a little faster and a lot louder. The listener had the urge to gesture with a roll of the hand and eyes and say, "Come on, out with it. You can do it."

While Sunset was a likeable person on screen and in person,

on occasion he seemed to get a streak of perceived injustice or an inclination to take people to court. One such person on the receiving end of this aspect of his personality was Jim Welch of South Carolina Educational Television and the series Sunset narrated for PBS. The dispute between them was settled but not before it caused some pain for both Welch and the cowboy star. Early in his career, he had disputes with the head of Republic Pictures and late in his career, litigation continued to raise its ugly head in connection with some low, low-budget films.

Sunset's parents gave him a name that would not stand up in Westerns. Maybe in the West but certainly not in shoot-em-ups. That handle was Winifred Maurice Harrison. Now how would you feel as a kid if you had to tell your school chums you had seen a Western over the weekend and it starred a guy named Winifred Maurice Harrison. Who??!!?? Not Roy and not Tex and not Gene but ...well, you know.

So young Sunset learned to ride a horse in either Oklahoma or Texas (maybe both), and he was so good that he picked up rodeo prizes. That, and his good looks, landed him in Hollywood and in a 1943 war-years United Artists movie titled STAGE DOOR CANTEEN. He was listed as Michael Harrison, and his character was a guy named Tex. It is said that this is a great film if for no other reason than to see the stars of the day and to be reminded of what it was like in World War II. The film is mostly about boosting morale during the war and about patriotism.

Our tall cowboy hero also appeared in a film called JANIE (Warner Bros., 1944) a year later and thereafter was the ride-like-the-wind guy we came to know and love. His early Westerns at Republic had Smiley Burnette listed as the lead, which was really unique. Can you imagine a Hoppy movie with Andy Clyde listed above William Boyd or a Don "Red" Barry film with Wally Vernon named as the star? OREGON TRAIL (Republic, 1945), by the way, featured some great scenes with one of my favorite badmen in Westerns, Tex Terry of Indiana. Other "badmen" who frequented the Sunset films included Roy Barcroft, Edmund Cobb, George Chesebro, Harry Woods, Tom London and Earle Hodgins.

In 1946, the Motion Picture Herald poll rankings had him listed as 8th. His pictures had the great production values of Republic, they had those aforementioned Republic badmen, and some of them had Peggy Stewart and Linda Stirling as leading ladies. Those were the Sunset Carson glory years, those very few years in the middle 1940s in Republic Westerns with the likes of Lesley Selander and Thomas Carr at the controls. After that, it would be down hill for our star, or up hill depending on your perspective. Never would such films as OUTLAW GRIZZLY, BATTLING MARSHAL, and MARSHAL OF WINDY HOLLOW (they couldn't even spell it right — they spelled it "Marshall" on the ads) come close to those at Republic. And somewhere in between the good and the bad films of Sunset Carson, the talented duo of Oliver Drake and Elmer Clifton could not rescue some of the cheap oaters.

Likewise, an appearance by the great Ken Maynard (another Indiana native) could not elevate the level of the WINDY HOLLOW movie. And Lash LaRue with Sunset in ALIEN OUTLAW was not a winning combo. A much more pleasing pairing of the two was when they were guest stars at the first Memphis Film Festival in 1972. That would have been a good one to attend because Russell Hayden and Don "Red" Barry showed up.

Now it's a jump from 1972 to 1989, but let me take a leap and say this: Sunset Carson looked great in 1989 when he appeared with Roy and Dale at the Portsmouth, Ohio gathering a year before his death. It was about as good as it gets in America when he stood tall and handsome at the Scioto County Fairgrounds in Southern Ohio and greeted a large crowd. Roy and Dale were there on the outdoor stage with him, and Old Grady had his trusty camera pointed at each of them. I think 1989 was the last time I saw Sunset in person. We shared correspondence during his rhubarb with Jim Welch, but I lost track of him during the final months before his death in Reno.

Many of you were very close to Sunset, much closer than me. I know because you have shared your stories with me. You may not know as much about him as do Boyd Magers, Bobby Copeland, and Richard B. Smith III, but it is my hope that you've shared some of your memories with this publication as I have. So long, pardners.

Minard Coons (a fan, and a musician): I was fortunate to do a couple shows with Art Davis, Louise Stanley and Sunset, in Greensboro, North Carolina. Sunset was going to do his shooting act, but the local police would not allow it. So Sunset did some recitations — one being "Cowboy Heaven" — a take off on Eddie Dean's "Hillbilly Heaven." Art and I played back-up for the song. It made me think of the time when I was with Sunset, after the accident, when the car hit him, we were all in a hotel, and Sunset told us he must have been nearly died at the time of the accident because he saw a corral with Art, Eddie Dean and all the cowboy movie stars. It was a pretty descriptive picture he painted — and a bit eerie.

Sunset "Kit" Carson
Sharp Shooters Club

THIS IS TO CERTIFY THAT

Mr. **Bobby Copeland**

IS A MEMBER IN GOOD STANDING

WNOW T.V. YORK, PA.

NORTH CAROLINA LEGAL PROBLEMS

(The following article, from a 1976 Greensboro, North Carolina newspaper, tells about the Greensboro City Council halting Sunset's shooting act.)

Shoot! Old Sunset Never Got To
by Jerry Kenion

All right, now partners, let's get this straight. The good guys wear white hats. The bad guys wear white hats. Right?

Cowboy star Sunset Carson wears a white hat. And Friday night, Sunset gave a black hat to the Greensboro city council. Sunset came to Greensboro to put on a Wild West shooting exhibition during the Carolina Film Festival now going on at the Carolina Theater. He came here at his own expense to help out in the effort to generate interest in saving the old theater.

Sunset never fired the first shot. Thursday, before Sunset's first stage show, someone filed a complaint. Because Greensboro has an ordinance against discharging firearms in the city, the police had to tell Sunset not to shoot. Kids and adults from as far away as Connecticut waited at the Carolina Theater Thursday, hoping that Sunset would win his battle with the ordinance. They were disappointed. The show didn't go on.

Friday the kids were back, getting autographs, having their pictures taken with the Western hero. And they were asking Sunset when he was going to show off his shooting skills. The kids were disappointed as Sunset had to tell one after another that he couldn't shoot in Greensboro. Here he was, this real-life rodeo champ who never met a foe he couldn't conquer on the screen — and he had to tell all those pleading kids there was nothing he could do about it.

Only the city council could rescue Sunset. Friday wore on and nothing happened. There was no go ahead. The ordinance stood, and it seemed that the city council had no plans to make any changes. And that is why the city council is now the owner of a black hat.

Bob Williams, one of the organizers of the Film Festival, laughingly said that the city council members were wearing black hats. Then, still laughing, Williams said that maybe council would get the message loud and clear if Sunset sent them a black hat. Williams vanished from the theater for a few minutes, and when he returned, he carried a brand spanking new black hat. Not only did he find the hat he had in mind, but the local haberdasher, Bob Blumenthal, thought the idea was so great that he donated the hat.

The kids in the theater caught on and enjoyed the whole thing. They gathered around Sunset as he held up the black hat and signed a picture: "To the Greensboro City Council. God bless you. Sunset Carson and fans."

Sunset Carson delivered the black hat to the police station about 7 p.m. Friday. A police spokesperson said that the city council's black hat can be claimed in the city manager's office.

SUNSET AT THE FESTIVALS

Sunset appeared at many of the Western film festivals around the country, and was always a fan favorite.

1986 Knoxville Film Festival. Buck Taylor, Jock Mahoney, Lash LaRue, Dub Taylor, Sunset, Peggy Stewart, Pierce Lyden.

Sunset and Peggy Stewart, circa 1976.

"Okay, boys, time's up!"

Famous B-Western books' author Buck Rainey with Sunset.

Sunset and son Michael.

THEY'RE WRITING ABOUT SUNSET

Barry Corbin (Sunset was also an inspiration to this current character actor): Sunset Carson was about to hit a guy and he ... did this (clenched his jaw muscle imitating Carson). I said "That's acting, so from then on, whenever I'll play cowboy, I'm going on like this (clenching his jaw muscle)." I just saw a Sunset Carson movie recently; he was not nearly as good an actor as I thought he was when I was eight. But he was still not bad.

Hans J. Wollstein (writing for the *All Movie Guide*): At the height of his screen career (1944-1946), American

RED RIVER RENEGADES (Republic, 1946)

RIO GRANDE RAIDERS (Republic, 1946)

Western star Sunset Carson ranked an impressive eighth in a national B-Western popularity poll, beating out most of the old-timers who had been around since the silent days. Handsome and boasting quite a following among female audience members — a rarity in the field of action adventures — Carson, alas, was also perhaps the era's least impressive thespian, and his time in the sun proved brief. The star claimed to have been named "All-Around Champion Cowboy of South America" in 1942, but like the earlier Tom Mix, Carson was no stranger to exaggerations. Signed by genre specialist Republic Pictures, the youngster was given a new moniker, Sunset Carson, and co-starred with former Gene Autry protégé Smiley Burnette in four well-received low-budget Westerns. Despite his lack of acting prowess, Carson looked great on a horse and was awarded his own series, beginning with SHERIFF OF CIMARRON (1945), directed by stunt expert Yakima Canutt. Sunset's vehicles benefited from generally good production values, pretty leading ladies who could also act (Linda Stirling and Peggy Stewart), and such solid character villains as Roy Barcroft and Kenne Duncan. Carson's uneasiness with dialogue, however, did not bode well for longevity, and he was summarily

fired by company boss Herbert J. Yates after reportedly showing up at a studio function inebriated and with an underage girl
on his arm. There would be a very low-budget series released
by a company known as Yucca Productions, but Carson was
basically a finished man in Hollywood after leaving Republic.
He would turn up in a couple of barely released low-budget
films — including the wretched sci-fi opus ALIEN OUTLAW
(1985) which also featured Lash LaRue — and was a frequent guest at B-Western fairs. But Carson is today perhaps
best remembered as the host of "Six Gun Heroes" a series of
B-Western revivals broadcast in the early 1980s by a South
Carolina public television station. A great deal heavier and still
having trouble delivering lines, Carson was, nevertheless, the
real McCoy, and the show remained successful for years.

BORDERTOWN TRAIL (Republic, 1944)

SANTA FE SADDLEMATES (Republic, 1945)

Don Miller (author of *Hollywood Corral):* Republic freaks would have voted Thomas Carr (director) a special Oscar for it (SANTA FE SADDLEMATES), had they the power — he began with three, count 'em three, fistic encounters, with Carson clobbering everybody in sight. With several more sessions of mayhem tossed in before the end, including one indulged in by heroine Linda Stirling, it was the fightin'est horse opera seen in many a moon.

James Horwitz (author of *They Went Thataway*): He was just a boy at the time. His films were an instant success. Even the girls liked Sunset. He was as handsome as hell and had a presence on the screen. He might have had a chance at a major studio. But Sunset was, perhaps, too young and too much of a country boy to make the most of his chance. They say he was wild and happy-go-lucky. That he drank to the point of outrage, and finally to oblivion. They say he threw it all away. Yet he was good. He could move. He could handle himself. He could ride. He could even act a bit. You could not say the thing same for Gene Autry. Sunset rose quickly in the ranks of cowboy heroes. And he fell just as fast and was washed up in pictures. But he remained a cowboy, which was what he knew best.

BOB BROWN REMEMBERS

Brown is often called the "Leonardo of Leather." He was a leather crafter for many years in Hollywood and crafted items for numerous Hollywood celebrities — particularly the cowboy stars. His recollection of Sunset may not be exactly precise.

Sunset Carson was my buddy for years. I met him in 1941 when he came into my shop. He introduced himself as Mickey Harrison, the all-around champion cowboy of the world for three years in Argentina. We were pals from the beginning. He said he loved the smell of leather. I furnished him my car most of the time. He had nothing; I took care of him for quite awhile. I took him out to Republic and got him signed on with old Pappy Yates. I furnished Sunset with my clothes to make him look good at Republic for his first starring picture, a Western of course.

Sunset liked to drink, I couldn't stop that. He got into a hell of a brawl at the bar on Vine and Hollywood Boulevard, called Sugar Hill. Eight rowdies called him a "slacker" because Sunset had a 4-F classification. They kept hounding him until he had enough. Sunset knocked one of them out. The other seven drunks at the bar mobbed Sunset. When the fight was over, Sunset had flattened six of them. One of them picked up a chair and broke it over Sunset's head. It was not a break-away chair either. He had to have his head and scalp sewed up with

36 stitches. Four of his front teeth were knocked out. I bought the bridgework that Sunset had to wear thereafter. Sometime later, his draft status was changed and he went into the Army. The training was too much for him, and he landed in the Army Hospital in Palm Springs where he spent six months.

He would write me every week from the hospital saying he was through with the movie business. He would say if he did make it out of the hospital, I would have to ride for him. It was a very sad time for Sunset. He was finally released, and he called me from the Hollywood Draft Office. He said, "Bobby, come and get me at the draft office at Santa Monica and Western Avenue." I jumped into my Buick and drove to the draft office. I parked at the foot of the staircase of the draft and looked up. There was Sunset waiting for me, dressed in house slippers and pajamas — no uniform, no duffle bag, and no nothing. He looked terrible. I said, "Wait for me." I ran up the long stairs, picked him up in my arms, and carried him down to my car. I took him to my shop on Hollywood Boulevard, fed him, and then took him home to where I lived with my mother.

Sunset stayed at our home for six months. I furnished him with my clothes, and my mother fed him good vegetables out of our garden to put weight on him. He only weighed about 140 pounds when I picked him up at the draft board. I bought him another partial plate of four teeth while he stayed with us.

He would play around with my horse Don for something to do; he wasn't able to ride yet. He finally said, "Bobby, I think I am ready to go back to Republic." The next day, I dressed him in my best clothes, and took him out to Republic and got him re-signed. He then made the best action pictures of all time.

When I left Hollywood in 1950 to join the Los Angeles County Sheriff's Office, it was because I couldn't get my money out of the studios. The end came to B-Westerns about this time, and Sunset went on the road with a circus, touring the world for years. I lost track of him for 30 years.

We met later in 1981 after all those years. He was in Nudie's tailor shop talking to Monte Hale. Monte told him I was alive and living in Big Bear City. Sunset couldn't wait to call me, and the next day he made the trip up to see me. From then on, I made all the artwork for Sunset's "Six Gun Heroes" and "Hollywood Nostalgia" videotapes, tee shirt designs, badges, holsters, attaché cases, etc. We picked up where we left off 30 years before, and then came his untimely death.

Sunset Carson poses for a publicity photo with female lead Linda Stirling on SANTA FE SADDLEMATES (Republic, 1945).

GOOD OLD BOY

There's no question that for years Sunset had a problem with alcohol, but, to his credit, he finally whipped it. And even when he was on the booze, he was a "good old boy." He had an unfailing love for his fans, and he was generous to a fault. It never was about money with Sunset but what he could do for others. Unlike today's film festival guest stars, Sunset would never have considered charging for an autograph or posing for a picture. Peggy Stewart said, "Sunset just lives to attend the festivals and seeing his fans." This is why that, no matter how many festivals he attended, he was always popular with the fans. I offer the following as evidence that shows he touched many lives in a positive manner:

While on a worldwide tour, the *Pacific Stars and Stripes* (authorized publication of the Armed Forces, Far East) wrote: *Cowboy hero Sunset Carson swore in more than 30,000 youngsters on Okinawa as members of his sharpshooting club during a live presentation of one of his shows on AFRTS TV station Okinawa. Sunset has added 20 million members to his fan club in the Far East. The membership cards and badges are furnished by different oil companies in Asia. Sunset is known throughout the Far East. "As the Cowboy Ambassador of Goodwill" originating from the many charity shows, he has given to help orphans and grief-stricken and hungry children, and to help build hospitals — Mr. and Mrs. Chiang Kai orphans in Formosa, typhoon victims in Japan, under-privileged children in Hong Kong and the Orthopedic Hospital in the Philippines. Sunset has never been known to refuse any deserving charity. Good luck, Cowboy, on your world tour.*

Many of the cowboys, including Roy Rogers, Gene Autry, Hopalong Cassidy, Buck Jones, and the Lone Ranger had a Cowboy Code for youngsters to follow. Sunset had what he called "The Sunset Carson Trail Blazers Code."

- I will obey my father and mother.
- I will study my lessons.
- I will be kind to animals.
- I will look before crossing the street.
- I will eat plenty of fruits and vegetables.
- I will drink my milk every day.
- I will go to bed early.
- I will love and obey my teacher.
- I will attend church and Sunday school.
- I will remember and obey the Ten Commandments.
- I will study and obey all traffic rules.

Sunset was often referred to as "The Cowboy Ambassador of Good Will," and for good reasons — because he never refused to perform on behalf of any deserving charity. When he started his "I said no to alcohol and drugs" Club, he wrote in one of the Club's newsletters, *"If we could just help one child, it would be worth it. I will fly in and bring membership badges and cards at my own expense. You furnish the hotel — fair enough?"* He gave away thousands of cards and badges at his own expense.

Positive Comments by Western Film Performers

Peggy Stewart: I absolutely adored Sunset. We had rapport as soon as we met. The thing I liked about him is, he never did really lose his innocence. From his toes to his ears, he had a great innocence. He wasn't innocent, of course, but he had child-like innocence that was very loveable.

Tom London: Sunset gave me the chance to play his sidekick; I will always be grateful to him for that.

Linda Stirling: How could you not like Sunset? I enjoyed working with him because we were both tall, and he was so sweet — kinda like an overgrown kid. We got along fine, and the films I made with him were fun. But I think he liked Peggy the best (Laugh).

Tex Terry (stuntman and minor player, often uncredited)**:** I worked quite a bit with Sunset Carson, He was just a big, old, overgrown kid, but I liked him a lot.

Kirk Alyn: I was from New York and knew nothing about horses. In fact, I was scared to death of them, but Sunset was a great rider, and he was fun to work with.

Pierce Lyden: He was always fun, irresponsible, happy, and a joy to be around. But I don't think he ever grew up; as Peggy Stewart said: "He needed mothering."

Lash LaRue: I never worked with Sunset, but I like him. I've had a lot of problems with a lot of people, but never with Sunset Carson. We've been together at several of the film festivals, and we got along fine. I always enjoy seeing the big guy.

Monte Hale: Old Sunset Carson, bless his heart; I just loved the big, old guy. He gave me my first job in pictures.

Thomas Carr: Sunset was an awfully sweet guy; he tried as hard as he could, and eventually worked into a pretty good Western star.

Tim McCoy: Sunset is a nice fellow. I never knew him very well, but what I saw of him I liked very much.

Tommy Scott: Sunset worked for me for quite a while. We got along fine, and I really liked the big fellow.

Positive Comments by Fans

Paul Isenhour (a fan): I grew up in Hickory, North Carolina, and went to a theater every Saturday to see a B-Western movie. While I liked all the cowboys, Sunset Carson was my favorite. I thought he had great screen charisma, and I liked the way he walked and talked.

Around 1970, a friend and I were traveling near Bristol, Tennessee, when we happened to notice a little carnival and a marquee advertising an appearance by Sunset "Kit" Carson. I had never heard Sunset called "Kit." But, when we went into the carnival, sure enough there was my childhood hero. The carnival had hired Sunset to put on a shooting demonstration with his rifle, and he awed the fans with his outstanding marksmanship.

I got an opportunity to talk with him, and told him he was my favorite cowboy. He thanked me and graciously spent time talking with me. Meeting Sunset was a thrill. I was pleased to discover that he was everything I had hoped he would be. He surely did not disappoint me in any way. He gave me a couple of souvenirs, and I left the carnival a happy man.

When I met Sunset again, it was like meeting an old friend. He had come to Hickory to start a TV program on the local station. He remained on the show for about a year.

To me, Sunset Carson was a wonderful man. I appreciate the attention he gave me, and I am proud to have known him. He was a special person in my life.

John Leonard (author *Wild Bill Elliott*): I saw him at two or three festivals in the 1970s and 1980s. I found him to be very friendly and nice. He was friendly and always willing to sign autographs for his fans.

Larry Blanks (member of the Williamsburg Film Festival): I had just gotten into film festivals around 1989 when I met Sunset and wife Jeannie here at the Atlanta Film Festival. My brother-in-law had a restaurant that all the stars were brought on Friday night, and Diane and I were seated next to Sunset and Jeannie and across from Lash. What a thrill for me to be having dinner with two of my cowboy heroes — it was my first film festival. We had an excellent conversation with Sunset that night, and he told me about the pending lawsuit with the South Carolina PBS station. It was a very pleasant evening, and we enjoyed it very much. Nine days later, we heard he had won his lawsuit and passed away within 24 hours of getting the news.

Merrill McCord (author): Although I talked with Sunset a number of times, I can only say what everyone else would say — that he always was friendly and polite and tried to answer all questions; and his Republic films had more action than any other B-Western series in film history. However, I have something that some others may not be aware of. I was born and reared in a small West Kentucky town named Hopkinsville. The town was a weekly stop on a circuit (lower tier, of course) of professional wrestling, which possibly was headquartered in Nashville. As a kid, I got caught up in the sport, or whatever you want to call it, and went almost every Wednesday night to the local armory to see the matches. To draw a larger crowd, the promoters in the late 1940s brought in two former cowboy stars as referees. They were Don Barry and Sunset. Each appeared only once in my hometown. My best guess on the date is 1947 or 1948.

Don Key (owner of Empire Publishing, and former publisher of *The Big Reel*): I thought Sunset was a nice man. He was kind to me and kind to a lot of other people. My first encounter with him was in 1976. By that time, I had been to three or four film conventions, and I thought I knew a little something about putting on a show. My friend Bob Williams and I decided to put on a convention at the Carolina Theater. And, if we made a profit, it would go towards the Arts Council that was in charge of restoring the theater. We knew we had to have movies and some guest stars because that is what the conventions were all about. One

Sunset made the cover of *The Big Reel* in 1984.

of the first stars we contacted was Sunset Carson who was living in the North Wilkesboro area — about 60 miles from Greensboro — where we were at the time. Sunset was more than willing to come to help us, and the Arts Council out. We got him a room at a local hotel and he was with us for about four days. Sunset really worked hard for us. He went far beyond what was expected of him. He was big hit with

Sunset with *The Big Reel* publisher, Don Key. Check out Key's snappy leisure suit.

the little kids. When the event was over and it

was time to settle up with him, we fully expected to pay him for his time. Imagine our surprise when he said, "Listen fellows, I did not do this for money; I did it for our friendship. I was really glad I could help out to put this program together." We invited two other guest stars, Louise Stanley and Art Davis — all genuinely nice people.

I had seen Sunset earlier. He was trying to make a go of a little western town in Franklin, North Carolina, called Gold City. It was there where I first saw him do his shooting act. I was really impressed with what he could do with a .22 rifle. He could perform magic from 50-60 feet away with the rifle. I thought it was a trick. I examined his rifle and didn't see how it could be anything but real.

Many of the Western actors were called "Drug Store Cowboys" because they did not have a lot of horse, gun, lasso or rodeo experience. But Sunset was real; he could do it all. I saw Sunset many more times, and I considered him a good friend.

Sunset is ready for his sharpshooting act with rifle.

SUNSET'S FILMS

Contributed by Paul Dellinger

In just two years, 1945 and 1946, Sunset Carson made more of an impression on Western filmdom than most cowboys managed in their entire movie careers. Those were the Republic years, in which the recently-dubbed Sunset starred in 11 actionful pictures, plus a guest stint in a Roy Rogers extravaganza. His introduction to movie audiences actually came in 1944 when he co-starred with Smiley Burnette as Sonny "Sunset" Carson. The odd pairing resulted in four pictures, the last of which is a comedy! After that, Smiley would depart from Republic forever, and Sunset would become the "main player" that we all knew he was, anyway.

As Michael Harrison, Sunset appeared in STAGE DOOR CANTEEN (United Artists, 1943) as a character named Texas, amid a star-studded cast of performers for servicemen. In JANIE (Warner Bros., 1944), a comedy about a girl (Joyce Reynolds) with a fondness for men in uniform, he played Sgt. Carl. In 1944, he tried out at Republic Studios, and found his niche — at least for the next few years. But, as mentioned, Sunset didn't begin as the star of his own pictures. Top billing went to Smiley Burnette, who had come to Republic with Gene Autry and co-starred with others including Roy Rogers and Bob Livingston while there. As the only comic sidekick to be elevated to top billing in a Western series, even if it was only four films, Smiley's roles were built up more than usual, but it was Sunset who carried the action. In each film, Smiley's character was named Frog Millhouse, while Sunset played Sunset, as he would do in all the rest of his Westerns.

The public got its first look at Sonny "Sunset" Carson in CALL OF THE ROCKIES (Republic, 1944), with Harry Woods supplying the villainy, Ellen Hall the beauty, and Kirk Alyn (best known for his "Superman" and "Blackhawk" serial roles at Columbia, although he would later do some Republic chapterplays, too) as a young mining engineer. Sunset alternated between the light cowboy shirt with the arrow pockets and the striped dark one, as he would do for the rest of his Republic stint. He wore a brace of stag-handled guns butts forward, Wild Bill Elliott-style. Film highlights include battles in the Republic cave set and some suspense as Sunset holds a gun on a renegade doctor (Frank Jaquet) to force him to save the life of a double-crossed outlaw (Tom London) who can expose the others. In his film, Smiley talks to the audience.

Next was BORDERTOWN TRAIL (Republic, 1944), in which Frog and Sunset are members of the Border Patrol, tracking smugglers led by outlaws Weldon Heyburn and Addison Richards. Sunset acquires his first brother in the Border Patrol commander, Vic Carson (Jack Luden), his only movie brother to survive at the end of the film. For unknown reasons, Luden's voice was dubbed.

(Note: Jack Luden starred in four Westerns for Columbia in 1938, and he is the only cowboy star to die in prison. Luden got into several scrapes with the law, initially in 1948 and again in 1950, and died of a heart problem in San Quentin Prison on February 15, 1951. He had been in the prison for slightly over eight months, serving time for issuing insufficient funds (bad checks) and a drug conviction (heroin). His occupation prior to his imprisonment was listed as "manager of a retail food store." Luden was cremated, and his ashes were reported to have been sent to his mother in Encinitas, California, in March of 1951.)

CODE OF THE PRAIRIE (Republic, 1944) gave Heyburn a sympathetic role this time, as Sunset's lawman friend even though he is temporarily duped by the bad guys until the final brief-but-blazing shoot-out when he and Sunset wipe out the entire gang. Tom Chatterton plays an aging ex-lawman named Bat Matson, no doubt inspired by the real-life Bat Masterson. But the most significant casting is Sunset's first encounter with resident Republic villain Roy Barcroft as the brains heavy and pretty Peggy Stewart as the leading lady. Sunset would see a lot of them both in future films.

In this unusual ending (probably not appreciated by the kids), Smiley turns directly to the audience and says, "You kids go home now. You've been in here all day."

In later years, Sunset described Barcroft off-screen as "my best friend," and he and Peggy were frequent co-stars at film festivals around the country. The last of the foursome was the outright Western comedy, FIREBRANDS OF ARIZONA (Republic, 1944), in which Smiley played a dual role as Frog and the notorious outlaw "Beefsteak Discoe." The movie ends with Smiley, as Beefsteak, and Sunset slugging it out and finally shooting it out after Sunset identifies the real Frog by the pills he is always taking. Peggy Stewart is back as a ranch owner who becomes disgusted with Frog's laziness and his excuses about feeling ill all the time. Later, she gets in on the horseback gunfighting right along with Sunset. Earle Hodgins plays a fast-talking sheriff who convinces Frog at one point that Frog is duty-bound to allow himself to be hanged, when he is mistaken for Beefsteak, so that the town can build a memorial to the famous outlaw. Barcroft is the sheriff's deputy, another switcheroo, and packs a pearl-handled pistol for perhaps the only time in his career.

At that point, Smiley moved over to Columbia where he would join Charles Starrett's *Durango Kid* series and eventually re-team with Gene Autry who had also migrated there. And Sunset moved to the top of his pictures' cast, starting with SHERIFF OF CIMARRON (Republic, 1945). The only cosmetic changes were a white bandana around the neck instead of the dark one of the earlier pictures, and a new brace of pearl-handled six-shooters in a gunbelt and holsters with even bigger studs than in the previous foursome.

Sunset plays a man who has completed a prison sentence for a crime he didn't commit. Although he doesn't find out until the end the real culprit was his kid brother, played by perennial kid Riley Hill, this time as a secret member of the outlaw band led by Jack Ingram. Hill, who would go on to define the hot-headed but honest kid roles in Monogram's Johnny Mack Brown and Jimmy Wakely Westerns, is utterly evil here. He even kills the father of leading lady Linda Stirling, who teams with Sunset for the first time.

Olin Howlin provides the comedy as a put-upon town veterinarian. In the first few minutes of the film, Sunset rides into town, has Linda topple off a stool and into his arms, fights off two of three would-be bank robbers, chases them all out of town before dropping two of them and capturing the third with his bullwhip (in a sequence that would be lifted for several other Sunset vehicles) — which is how he becomes the movie's title character. Maybe the fact that the movie was directed by veteran stuntman Yakima Canutt helped.

It was also here that Sunset established his character as a somewhat flirtatious cowboy hero. Not only did he trick the heroine into falling off a stool so he could catch her, but he clicks his tongue at her in a way she appears to find insulting. (The sound is more often associated with signaling a horse to speed up.) In the movie, the father of Linda Stirling's character finds it all highly amusing.

But if audiences thought SHERIFF OF CIMARRON was full of action, they got even more with SANTA FE SADDLEMATES (Republic, 1945). Sunset has three different fights before the plot even gets under way to test his mettle for the assignment. It turns out Lash LaRue would use the same scenario a few years later in OUTLAW COUNTRY (Western Adventure,

1949). Next, he takes on some saloon toughs when one of them (Bud Geary) tries to get too friendly with singer Linda Stirling (an undercover newspaper reporter). Finally, he and "saddlemate" Olin Howlin (playing a dude wanting to be a cowboy) infiltrate the gang of smugglers led by Roy Barcroft and smash them.

Johnny Carpenter is a member of the gang, and Kenne Duncan plays the gunfighter whom Sunset has been impersonating. This movie moved so fast that the heroine's name is never even mentioned, not even by the time she and Sunset are becoming friskily romantic at the end. Thomas Carr had become Sunset's director, and would direct all the rest of the big cowboy's films at Republic.

(Eagle-eyed Richard B. Smith III spotted several boo-boos in the movie: (1) leading lady Linda Stirling's character name is never revealed; (2) when Carson is ordered by governor Frank Jaquet to report for a meeting with him in room 211, there is no number on the door when he enters after concluding a fight scene with George Magrill; (3) finishing a segment with new partner Olin Howlin outside the saloon, the gun handle on Carson's right-holstered pistol appears noticeably bent and extremely tarnished, yet just a few frames later has been corrected; (4) once gang head Roy Barcroft gives directions to a ranch and points out his place of business at a considerable distance down the Republic street but not identifying himself, Carson, however, addresses Barcroft personally with his character name in a later scene; (5) Carson retrieves a white hat from bushes which he places in his left saddlebag partially exposed yet moments afterwards while on horseback the hat has disappeared from view; and (6) behind a corral fence adjacent to the famous Republic Duchess barn-ranch house complex, an automobile is visible driving through rear woods as one player speaks dialogue.)

In OREGON TRAIL (Republic, 1945), Carr's mother — former silent film actress Mary Carr — gets to play a character role as Peggy Stewart's feisty grandmother (who even gets involved in the final gunfight). Sunset becomes sheriff again, has another shoot-out with Kenne Duncan (after being shot in the back and hospitalized by Duncan), and uses a bullwhip to pull a would-be stage robber off his horse. This time there is no comic sidekick at all. Both Monte Hale and Rex Lease are billed but cut from the release print.

BANDITS OF THE BADLANDS (Republic, 1945), sees Sunset as a ranger who plans to take the law into his own hands when he finds the killer of his doctor/brother (played by Monte Hale). He does this by infiltrating an outlaw town with stage driver Si Jenks, and finds Peggy Stewart and her gunsmith father virtual prisoners there. Alerted by Stewart's character that has fallen for Sunset, the rangers arrive on the scene in time to keep Sunset from murdering the man he has finally hunted down. For some reason, Sunset was relegated to packing only one pearl-handled six-gun this time. And except for his next picture, he would be a one-gun hero for the rest of his Republic stint.

This is also the film where Sunset has a problem with a word in the script. After he has stopped a stage and is ready for it to roll again, he says, "Wind them wheels" ("wind" being like a breeze). Director Tommy Carr yelled, "Cut! Sunset, it's 'Wind them wheels!' ("wind" as wind up a clock). Sunset says, "Well, damn, it looks like wind (breeze) to me."

That next picture was ROUGH RIDERS OF CHEYENNE (Republic, 1945), an almost "Romeo and Juliet" horse opera with feuding families, the Stirlings and the Carsons. Interestingly, Melinda Stirling is played not by Linda Stirling but by Peggy Stewart, and her Lady MacBeth-like mother by Mira McKinney. Sunset is drawn into the feud to avenge the killing of his father (Eddy Waller, future "Nugget Clark" in the Rocky Lane series), and ably assisted by ranch foreman Monte Hale, who gets to sing the only song to grace a Sunset Carson film. Hale's character later dies protecting Sunset, and Sunset nearly guns down Stewart who has disguised herself as her brother to save him from a shoot-out with Sunset. But

Sunset ferrets out the real culprits and brings peace to Paradise Valley. Once again, the action is all that fans expected from the Carr and Carson team. Monte Hale has a good supporting role in one of his several pre-starring days' films.

The last picture of the 1945 season was THE CHEROKEE FLASH, with the surprise casting of Roy Barcroft as not only a good guy but Sunset's father, and the title character as well. Once an outlaw known as the Cherokee Flash, Barcroft has reformed and resists efforts by his old gang to bring him back into the fold. He and Sunset, with Tom London supplying the sidekick honors, do that in style while Linda Stirling does leading lady honors this time around.

Sunset also appeared during 1945 in the Roy Rogers vehicle, BELLS OF ROSARITA, in which Roy and The Sons of the Pioneers enlist a line-up of Republic movie stars in this modern Western to help save Dale Evans' and Gabby Hayes' circus by guest appearances. Sunset answers the call along with Allan Lane, Robert Livingston, Don Barry and "Wild Bill" Elliott. They also join Roy in rounding up the outlaw gang at the end. "Let's get 'em, boys," calls Roy. "They're rationed — one to a man." But the funniest line in the picture has to be from henchman Roy Barcroft when he and villain Grant Withers find their car missing: "There must be some crooks around here!" Sunset has an action scene filming a fight at Republic when he gets Roy's call for help (although this is cut from some versions of the film) and is the first of the guest stars to "get his man" at the end, riding after him and stopping him with a bullwhip before jumping down and clobbering him.

Sunset's horse is identified in the movie as Silver. During an appearance at Hillbilly World, Tennessee, in the early 1970s, as Sunset "Kit" Carson, he told this writer that his horse was to have been Buck Jones' new Silver, had Jones not been killed in a tragic fire, and that Sunset said he dropped the name "Silver" because of that "Hi Yo Silver stuff with the Lone Ranger." He renamed the white horse Cactus.

(Note: In at least one of his independent outings, the color version of BATTLING MARSHAL (Yucca, 1950), his horse is billed as "Cactus Jr." but appears to be a palomino.)

The 1946 Republic season opened with DAYS OF BUFFALO BILL, which had nothing whatever to do with Bill Cody, but had Sunset mistakenly believing he'd shot and killed Peggy Stewart's brother. He and sidekick Tom London try to make up for things by helping her save her ranch, although later she almost shoots Sunset when she finds out who he is. Sunset eventually clears himself and rounds up the outlaws. Oddly, there's no mention of "Buffalo Bill" or his "Days" in the movie.

ALIAS BILLY THE KID (Republic, 1946) likewise has nothing to do with Billy Bonney, but has Sunset as a ranger infiltrate Peggy Stewart's outlaw gang only to find his sympathies with her and against cattle broker Roy Barcroft. Tom Keene, Buck Jones (in Columbia's 1931 THE TEXAS RANGER) and George O'Brien, Rita Hayworth and Tim Holt (in RKO's 1938 THE RENEGADE RANGER) had all done it before, but it was still a serviceable plot. This was the beginning of Sunset's references to Peggy Stewart as "baby sister," which she pretended to be in the script to get one of her men out jail. Eventually, Sunset clears Stewart's followers and jails Barcroft, and all is right with the world once more.

After going undercover as an outlaw in so many movies, Sunset really is an outlaw in THE EL PASO KID (Republic, 1946), but breaks with the gang led by Robert Filmer, when it won't help its wounded old-timer member Hank Patterson. The two ex-gang members plan to begin their own outlawry, but the sheriff's daughter (diminutive Marie Harmon, Sunset's only other Republic leading lady besides Stewart and Stirling) sees them drive off their rivals in a stage holdup attempt and embarrasses them into changing their ways. Sunset actually becomes a deputy, although he is still playing a waiting game until he can make a big score. Eventually, he does move over to the side of Right and wins both a pardon and the girl.

Tom London is back again as the sidekick in RED RIVER RENEGADES (Republic, 1946), a mystery about vanishing stagecoaches, but London is actually the senior postal inspector. Ed Cobb, who played the competent sheriff of EL PASO KID, is working with undercover Pinkerton detective Peggy Stewart here. But all the undercover operatives keep stumbling over one another in their search for the real crooks before everything is straightened out.

Sunset's farewell Republic opus was RIO GRANDE RAIDERS (Republic, 1946) in which he gets yet another brother, played by none other than Bob Steele. This time, Sunset's brother is the ex-con and falls into bad company among outlaws led by Tris Coffin. Carson and Steele end up as rivals in a stagecoach race, but Steele changes sides in time to stop a fatal bullet and Sunset avenges him in a shoot-out. Linda Stirling is back one last time as the leading lady, who rides off with Sunset aboard a stagecoach for a wedding. Sunset and Bob Steele made an odd pairing for brothers, considering Sunset's height and Bob Steele's short stature. But Steele capitalized on the seeming oddity by constantly referring to Sunset as "Shorty." The narrator for the movie is perennial badman LeRoy Mason.

(Note: Some thought it ridiculous casting by having Bob Steele play Sunset's brother, since Sunset is over a foot taller than Steele. However, Steele's real-life twin brother, William Bradbury, was some eight inches taller than Bob.)

Researcher Richard B. Smith III adds: Despite this unfortunate turn of events in his life (losing his contract at Republic), Sunset would later derive a great deal of personal pride when Life magazine (10/7/46) afforded RIO GRANDE RAIDERS a seven-page photo feature with information compiled during the oater's filming (7/8/46 through 7/15/46) at approximately $35,000. The extensive write-up served as a typical example of how a B-hayburner was lensed in the 1940s. Twenty-six photos were juxtaposed to lend credence for the article. Included were: two pictures of Carson decking badman Kenne

Duncan; Sunset on the receiving end of bullets bouncing off a building wall which were actually gelatin capsules fired by the prop man from a special air-pressure gun; film editor William Thompson choosing stock footage — 20% of RIO GRANDE RAIDERS for the final print; a slingshot utilized by an off-camera person to smash a light bulb supposedly done by a bullet shot in Carson's direction; Sunset's bullwhipping a pistol from player George Bell's hand; a full-page shot of Carson inside a sound stage sitting on the stagecoach driver's seat against a process screen as the prop man shakes the vehicle to suggest a rough ride while another person rattles foliage before a light as a shadow effect; veteran Bob Steele shooting at a thrown trick bottle, which succeeds once a special effects man ignites a charge inside the glass itself. Director Tommy Carr shot off the cuff rather than follow an assigned script. Carr consumed most of his time instructing 15 actors when to shoot it out. Republic rented Iverson's Ranch for one day at $100 and instructed the company not to intermingle with actors working simultaneously on two other Westerns. The remaining five days had actors/technical crew going through their paces on the back lot. RIO GRANDE RAIDERS required nearly 67 setups per day to keep pace with its frantic schedule and was expected to gross $52,000 in box-office receipts. Several reverse close-up shots of Steele driving a stage can be eyed. Stock footage inserted includes Republic's RHYTHM OF THE SADDLE (1938) and its serial ADVENTURES OF RED RYDER (1940).

It would not be until 1947 that Sunset began his new low-budget — really low — at so-called Astor Pictures, also known as Yucca Productions. The casts were mostly unfamiliar with leading lady Pat Starling hardly able to measure up to Stewart and Stirling or even Harmon. Steven Keyes as Sunset's most frequent adversary was no Barcroft, either. Young Al Terry (sometimes credited as Al Terr) had a few sympathetic roles as a youngster, but it never quite jelled for audiences used to Republic standards. In SUNSET CARSON RIDES AGAIN (1947), the picture did have left-handed heavy Bob Cason as the leading villain and was in color with Sunset as a ranch owner.

DEADLINE (1948) makes him a Pony Express rider, FIGHTING MUSTANG (1948) puts him back in the rangers, BATTLING MARSHAL (1950) makes him (what else?) a marshal, and 1949's RIO GRANDE (not to be confused with the John Wayne/John Ford picture) makes him a cowboy. All but the last were directed by veteran Oliver Drake, but it didn't help.

Sunset managed to get two other films made — OUTLAW GRIZZLY in 1971 and MARSHAL OF WINDY HOLLOW in 1972 which featured an elderly Ken Maynard as the Texas Ranger that sends Sunset on his mission. Neither film was ever released. In 1977, Sunset played a supporting role in BUCKSTONE COUNTY PRISON, also known as "Seabo" (the lead character's name) as a lawman sending bounty hunter Earl Owensby (as Seabo, and who also owned the studio where the film was made) on his mission. Don Barry is effective as a crooked prison warden. In 1985, Sunset and Lash LaRue play supporting roles in a low-budget sci-fi opus called ALIEN OUTLAW.

Leading lady Pat Starling and Sunset Carson take a breather in 1947 while shooting BATTLING MARSHAL (Yucca, 1950).

He was a frequent guest at Western film conventions around the country until his death May 1, 1990, in Reno, Nevada, leaving a legacy of some of the most actionful Westerns ever turned out by the actionful Republic.

The promotional photos of Sunset's later 1940s Yucca color movies were like the Westerns themselves – lousy.

SUNSET IN THE COMIC BOOKS

Thanks to Lansing Sexton

Sunset Carson's comics career began in Charlton's *Cowboy Western Comics* #27 dated August 1950. It features a photo cover and an adaptation of his Astor film SUNSET CARSON RIDES AGAIN (1947). Although specific adaptations do occur in Western hero comics, they are not the rule. This series is somewhat unusual in its adaptation of all of Sunset's Astor films. Issue 28 adapts both BATTLING MARSHAL (1950) and FIGHTING MUSTANG (1948). Issue 29 adapts RIO GRANDE (1949) as well as James Stewart's WINCHESTER 73 (Universal, 1950) and features a five-page biography of Sunset. Issue 30 has an adaptation of DEADLINE (1948). Issues 30 and 35 have photo covers, and the latter also has a photo on the inside front. Sunset was still featured in issue #37. I'm not sure about issues #38 and #39, but he was definitely out with issue #40 which became *Space Western Comics*. Charlton also published *Sunset Carson* comics, beginning with #1 dated February 1951. Only four issues were published. Issue #1 has a retouched photo cover rather like a painting, while #2 and #4 have drawn covers. All four issues have a black and white photo medallion of Sunset in the upper left corner.

This page and the next show examples of Sunset Carson comic book covers.

REPLACING TIM McCOY

Article from the *Piedmont Herald*

(Toccoa, Stephens County, Georgia — November 22, 1973)

Sunset Carson visited Stephens County on Monday of this week. Carson, the star of almost 70 movies, was on hand to make final plans with Tommy Scott to replace Col. Tim McCoy on Scott's traveling "Family Fun Time" and "Wild West Show" during the month of April. Col. Tim McCoy, billed as the "Original Real McCoy" and star of numerous movies is going to take the month of April for an around-the-world cruise. Scott stated that Col. McCoy had been with the show for the past 11 years, and "this is the first vacation he's had."

Tommy Scott, known as "Rambling Tommy Scott" to many Stephens Countians, brought his show into headquarters at Eastanollee for the 39th time this past Sunday. Scott's tours included most states and Mexico and Canada. Scott and Carson were on hand for a press conference at the Scott's home in Eastanollee. Both seemed to enjoy reliving some of the humorous and some of the not-so-humorous things that have happened to them in show business.

Scott recalled how he began by joining a medicine show as a guitar player. He later worked as a ventriloquist with his dummy "Luke McDuke." Carson is presently under contract with Warner Brothers to make pictures. His career in movies started in the early 1940s. He was starring in movies at the age of 16. Carson talked about his part in the show, "Most people see trick shots in the movies that they figure are fake shots, but I actually do it right out there in front of them on stage." His act includes shooting cigarettes from mouths, William Tell (shooting apples off someone's head), etc. He demonstrated part of his act by shooting balloons out of the mouths of Scott and his wife Frankie. Carson will open with the show in Seneca, South Carolina on April 1. He will also play the show in Elberton, Commerce, Winders and Rome.

(Note: Carson did not make almost 70 movies; he did not appear in films at 16; and was not under contract to Warner Bros. to make pictures.)

Tim McCoy

SUNSET'S LETTER
FOR TIM HOLT DAY

Tim Holt lived in Hurrah, Oklahoma in his later years. The city designated September 13, 1976, as "Tim Holt Memorial Day", and invited several Westerns stars to attend. Sunset sent the following letter:

Sunset Carson
P. O. Box 3751
Carroll Reece Station
Johnson City, Tennessee 37601
(615) 477 3062

September 10, 1975

Mr. Carl Knox
4524 NW 46th Street
Oklahoma City, Oklahoma 71322

Dear Mr. Knox,

Memory of Tim Holt stirs deep emotions in all of us who knew him. Most significantly are respect for the warm human kindness Tim radiated, humility for having been so fortunate as to have enjoyed the Acting Profession he so aptly served, profound admiration of the man himself, and affection for a good friend.

Many people live quietly and unnoticed, while others go to great length to be spectacular. Tim was an example of quiet greatness.

He did not strive to be spectacular, but the way that the natural warmth of his personality influenced all who passed his way is far from unnoticed.

Tim's talent, kindness, and genuine sincerity will be deeply missed by all of us fortunate as to have been his friends.

I sincerely offer my best wishes and kindest regards to his family, friends, and countless fans of this fine American on this memorial occasion.

Sincerely,
Sunset Carson

Tim Holt, probably in a studio publicity shot taken at RKO Radio Pictures around 1947.

FILM FESTIVAL FRAUDS

Many times, unscrupulous film festival promoters have attempted to lure fans to their events by advertising cowboys who have not even been invited to attend. In 1976, Sunset headed up a group of Western performers to try and stop such fraudulent ads. Below is an article by Kid Chissel that appeared in *Hollywood Independent* on April 29, 1976.

A "war council" was recently conducted in the spacious home of Carruth Byrd, spearheaded by Al Minto, regarding the "misuse" of veteran cowboys' names in various Western film festival events which have been taking place throughout the nation.

Heading the council meeting was Sunset Carson, Western hero in nearly 50 films, and who, in 1974, was given an award as one of the greatest cowboy heroes of all time, ranking in popularity through a public opinion poll only second to Gene Autry.

(Note: It would be interesting to see where this poll was taken.)

The purpose of the meeting was to meet with all available Western stars that have formed as an organization called "The

Movie Cowboy Association." In the meeting, Sunset discussed, with other prominent Western stars and producers, the fact the names of many Western stars are being used to promote these various "Western Festivals" which allegedly announce in their advertising by innuendo that certain Western stars will be appearing at certain festivals.

Many of the group there that night, which included Chill Wills, Monte Hale, Don "Red" Barry, Ben Johnson, and Peggy Stewart agreed that on many such occasions their names were advertised, but they were never invited to attend — either for free or for pay.

Chill Wills, however, told about a recent film festival in Florida where he was invited and the promoters, according to him, did not even pay his per diem or plane fare which resulted in his taking legal action.

Snuff Garrett passed around circulars which advertised a forthcoming Western West Coast Film Festival to be held in the middle of June at the Biltmore Hotel. It listed the names of 66 heroes, sidekicks, leading ladies and villains (including some dead!) and five of the above names at the meeting which had not even been informed. Then Sunset introduced a resolution that was agreed upon by all: the Western stars would appear at any of these festivals, providing that they were legitimate in furnishing proper housing and transportation, and donate their "fee" to the Motion Picture County Home.

After all, Sunset said, "These promoters charge $2.50 to $15 a person, sometimes even more, run our old films and even sell photographs of us which they have no right." Sunset went on and added, "They're not violating the law or doing anything illegal, but they should not use the names of the living cowboys to infer to the public that some of these Western stars will be there in person. It should be spelling out whether or not the stars will attend — and if so — their names and on what day. Most of this advertising in the past has been very misleading. Some of these have even announced that that certain Western *stars will be there in person and then later announce that "so" and "so" just couldn't make it — when the Western star was never really contacted at all."*

Don "Red" Barry called it a "rip-off."

Unanimously, the Western stars agreed to cooperate with these events, if their appearances were warranted, and if the proceeds could be donated to the Motion Picture County Home. It only sounds fair and could even be of greater advantage to promoters of such festivals. Other Western stars not in attendance but who were called and gave their support to this meeting were Rory Calhoun, James Craig, Iron Eyes Cody, Kirk Alyn, and Rand Brooks. Spencer Gordon Bennet, veteran

Don "Red" Barry

director of some of the screen's most exciting Western serials and features could not attend but agreed to the premise — so did producer Ed Finney.

The list of signatures is still growing and, in the future, all such festivals will have to deal with the newly formed "Movie Cowboy's Association" who will "clear" all such arrangements and cooperate with the festivals.

SUNSET CARSON DAY

Article from the *Plainview Daily Herald,* July 7, 2005

Olton, Texas Plans a Salute to Former Western Star Sunset Carson

OLTON — Aug. 6 has been proclaimed as "Sunset Carson Day" in Olton by Mayor Johnny Adams to salute a former Western movie star who lived near Olton as a child. The date coincides with the city's annual Sandhills Celebration, which was begun to recognize pioneers that settled this area.

There have been a number of events scheduled to pay honor to the memory of Winfred Maurice "Mickey" Harrison who lived about four miles east of Olton as a young boy. He was born in Gracemont, Okla. in 1920 or 1922.

Harrison, who visited relatives in this area several times, died May 1, 1990, in Reno, Nevada, took up acting at the suggestion of silent movie star Tom Mix. His first appearance was as Michael Harrison in the 1943 picture, "Stage Door Canteen," as a character named Texas. He would go on to star in 14 (actually 15) B-Westerns for Republic Pictures from 1944-45 (actually 1944-46).

At 10 a.m. Saturday, Aug. 6, members of Carson's family and friends, who have traveled to Olton to pay tribute to him, will *ride in the annual parade.*

The dedication of a memorial plaque to Sunset Carson will be held under an open air pavilion in downtown Olton, at the corner of 9th and Main at 1 p.m., when all Sandhills honorees will be recognized.

Plans are to introduce John Buttram (Pat Buttram's nephew), a close friend; Marie Harmon, leading lady in the movie "El Paso Kid"; and all others that traveled from a long distance to participate in the event. They will each be given an opportunity to talk about their memories of Sunset Carson.

The memorial plaque will then be taken to the Sand Crawl Museum for its permanent place outside the museum.

A theater room, which holds memorabilia of Sunset Carson, will be the next stop of the tour. There are dozens of pictures, movie posters, newspaper articles and DVDs for showing his old movies. Movies may be viewed by those visiting or just browsing through the articles on display.

Attending "celebrities" will offer autographed pictures they had made with Sunset Carson.

Sue Cannon, former editor and publisher of the Olton Enterprise who is helping to stage the event, remarked: "This is the first time we have ever done anything like this and we are very inexperienced in putting on this type of event. We need suggestions to

Caption: Plaque honoring Sunset at the Olton, Texas, Sand Crawl Museum.

make it better. We are looking forward to meeting all these people who are coming to pay tribute to Sunset."

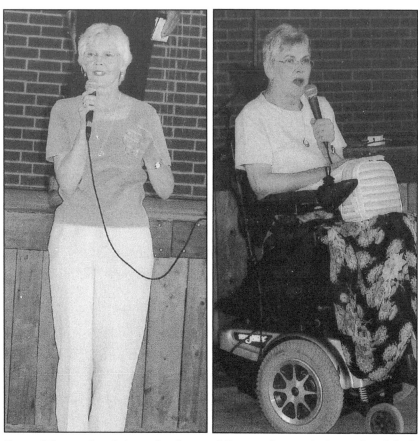

Two of Sunset's sisters: Azalee and Peggy. Peggy is in a wheelchair due to having polio.

THE ASTOR PICTURES FROM YUCCA/LAUTEM

Oliver Drake (After being approached by producer Walt Mattox regarding Drake's directing a series of Sunset Carson films): *When he showed me the budget, I backed away and said, "You can't make a good Western on that kind of money. It's impossible."*

Walt headed back in his chair, grinning smugly. "I'm not hiring you because I think you are the best director in the business, I'm hiring you and your ranch and your "Beasties" (a group of character actors that hung around Drake's ranch). *I'll pay everyone the lowest union scale, sign scale contracts, and let them defer the rest of their usual salary." I thought it over, and it was a reasonable idea. I needed work so badly. We shook hands, and I walked out, wondering just what kind of situation I was getting into.*

On one occasion, we were getting ready to shoot a fight sequence on the desert near the ranch. It was early in the morning, and the crew and cast were preparing for the action. The fight scene was to take place between Steve Keyes and Sunset. Steve was playing a heavy in the picture. Then Sunset's flashy Cadillac pulled into the parking area and stopped nearby. Bob Cason, one of the heavies in the picture and also a fine stuntman, opened the driver's door and stumbled drunkenly out to open the rear door. Ice and beer cans spewed out from the rear floor of the Cadillac onto the ground. Sunset got out of the passenger's side and walked around the car. He stared at the mess and then at Cason. "What the hell have you done, Bob?" Guiltily, Bob grinned, "I thought we'd need some cool drinks," he mumbled, and started to pick up the cans and put them back into the car. I walked over to the car and eyed them coldly. Sunset grinned rather foolishly, and Bob didn't know what to say. I called Charlie Gould (assistant director) over: "Take this drunken character into the house and sober him up. We'll double Cason until he's able to get on the set."

Don Miller (author of *Hollywood Corral*): *Sunset Carson Westerns, once the pride of Republic, were now the scourge of Astor Pictures. Astor was an independent clearing house for assorted oldies and shoestring independent productions. Carson had signed with producer Walt Mattox to make a few Yucca Productions. Yucca was right.*

The films directed by Oliver Drake were terrible. DEADLINE (1948) was the most professionally made technically and the worst. Whatever possessed Drake to stretch the narrative by inserting interminable shots of Carson and heroine Pat Starling galloping along cannot be fathomed, but the results induced a state of torpor bordering on the mesmeric. If the ennui drove one's focus upon Miss Starling, her body movements caused a rhythmic pace of the steed became erotic — not enough to compensate for the other indelicacies, but a temporary stimulant. Besides, Starling was stacked.

On the other hand Carson, a towering 6-footer plus, was given opponents well below average height, and Sunset was hard put to make the brawls realistic. He exerted himself mightily to make the odds appear even, but the shrimps he battered about took the pummeling like so many bantam dolls. Carson's other three for Yucca weren't as tedious as DEADLINE, but were saddled with productions of the backyard variety. Carson starred in one more independent production filmed in Texas and also distributed by Astor, RIO GRANDE (1949). It was strictly amateur night.

MARSHAL OF WINDY HOLLOW

by Jerry Whittington

(In the early 1970s, Hal Miller and Jack Cates arranged the financing for a low-budget Western starring Sunset Carson with supporting roles for Tex Ritter (as the Mayor) and Ken Maynard (as a Texas Ranger). Jerry Whittington directed and did the film editing. Co-producers were Sunset Carson, Cates, and Miller.)

Director Jerry Whittington writes the following remembrance of the filming: *We shot the film in July of 1972, using 16mm film, at Windy Hollow which is about 10 miles south of Owensboro, Kentucky. Windy Hollow was the site of coal strip mining years ago. The mining left canyons that looked like Utah with water rushing through them — a great set for a Western like the ones shot in the 1930s and 1940s. We used 16mm for cost reasons, as the film stock and processing was significantly less than 35mm. And the 16mm camera and equipment was more portable than 35mm gear.*

We picked up all the old cowboy stars at the Evansville, Indiana airport. Ken Maynard, we didn't know, had a long beard, and we had to cut it off for the part he played as a

Texas Ranger. Hal Miller was the owner of Windy Hollow and the film's backer. The Western town he built for the film was great — saloon, bank, hotel, general store and all. There was a Western museum in the town, and all the cowboy stars had their picture taken in the museum with their posters and lobby cards. Ken Maynard brought a pair of his boots, shirt, pants and his hat he used in his old Westerns to give to the Museum.

The first day on the set Sunset Carson gave us a tour of the locations. We couldn't believe our eyes, as it looked just like the old B-Western locations of years ago. The filming equipment had not arrived as yet so we blocked out the shots with the script. There was an old restaurant at the end of the town set where we grubbed out every day. On our way to the airport to

Note the misspelling of Marshal in the title. Ken Maynard and Sunset Carson converse during footage for the unreleased MARSHAL OF WINDY HOLLOW (1972). That's a bit player dressed as an Indian chief. It's certainly not Iron Eyes Cody.

pick up the stars, we passed fire trucks. Sunset Carson said: "I hope the Western town is not on fire." Well just about when we got back to the restaurant, it had burned to the ground and a lot of 16mm films of Sunset Carson, Ken Maynard, and Tex Ritter etc. were lost in the fire.

The fire set us back a little, but we used a chuck wagon like they used in the old Westerns to cook the meals for the cast and crew. The cooking that was seen in the film was our meals. You couldn't get much "realer" than that — a lot of beans and cornbread — I got sick of them.

There was a lady that slept in her car for four nights before we started shooting the film. I got up the courage to ask her who she was — she said "I'm Bessie Maynard, Ken Maynard's sister ... I haven't seen him in over 35 years ... I drove here from Columbus, Indiana to see him." She said she didn't have the money to spend on a motel room, so the film crew chipped in and got her a room with Ken so she could be with him while he was on the shoot. She was with him every day on the set. What a joy it was to see them together after 35 years. Ken Maynard died about six months later back in California.

I think the whole State of Kentucky came to watch the filming and get parts in the film. We had 27 covered wagons in one scene. Every July, Hal Miller, the owner of Windy Hollow, had a wagon train show, and everybody was invited to bring their wagons and be in the film. They came from all over the states, and we had that chuck wagon fired up to feed all the people.

Film collectors and movie buffs came from all over the U.S. to see the filming when we did the big wagon train shot and pushed several over a cliff into the water, destroying four wagons; there were over 10,000 people there to see the filming. I never saw so many people on a movie set in the 40 years I worked on films. The local TV stations had on their news that we were going to do the big scene on July 4, 1972. Hal Miller had a big camp ground on the Windy Hollow grounds, and it was full of campers and motor homes

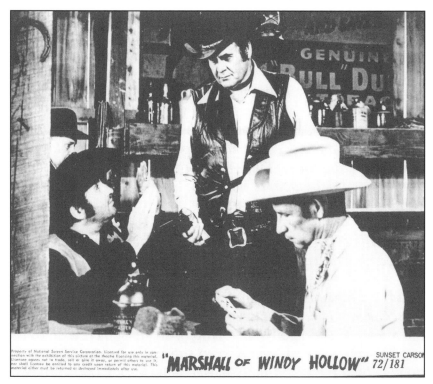

Property of National Screen Service Corporation. Licensed for use only in connection with the exhibition of this picture at the theatre licensing this material.
Licensee agrees not to trade, sell or give it away, or permit others to use it,
nor shall licensee be entitled to any credit upon return of this material. This
material either must be returned or destroyed immediately after use.

"MARSHALL OF WINDY HOLLOW" SUNSET CARSON 72/181

Sunset Carson grimly points his gun at an unknown player during a saloon segment from MARSHAL OF WINDY HOLLOW (1972).

from everywhere. That night, Tex Ritter and his band played for the hundreds of cast and crew of the wagon scene, and a lot of the crowd stayed also to see Tex Ritter sing.

The film was shot in 12 days just like the old B-Westerns of the 1930s and 1940s. We shot it in 16mm color and did some slow motion shots of the wagons going over the cliffs, outlaws being shot and falling into the water, and then we blew up the outlaw's shack and a barn. The film was full of action just like all of Sunset Carson's films.

Tex Ritter was great to work with. It was a treat to see Ken Maynard. He signed one of his 8x10 pictures for me that came from my uncle's theatre back in 1945 when he and his horse Tarzan did a personal appearance. By the way, I pinned the last sheriff's badge on Ken Maynard — it was a

Daviess County (Kentucky) sheriff's badge, and I forgot to get it back from Ken before he left to go back to California.

When I completed the editing, Hal Miller and Jack Cates came to High Point, North Carolina, from Owensboro, Kentucky, and picked up the film (which was on A-rolls and B-rolls and title rolls with all sound tracks and special EFX sound tracks ready to be printed at the lab). Jack Cates was to take the film to the MPL Labs in Memphis for printing and processing into a complete 16mm print ready for showing. I recall that Cates was also to pay the cost of this 16mm color print (the cost of a timed, color corrected release print in 1972 was about 75 cents a foot or around $3,000.00).

That was the last I saw of the MARSHAL OF WINDY HOLLOW. It was never released, and the whereabouts of the film is still a mystery to me.

If the finished film was not properly stored for all these years, the hot glue splices in the A and B rolls would be brittle and loss of color at the splices and the film warp could make it no good for completing the 16mm release print. The film would have to be printed with all the rolls. And the mag sound track rolls would have to be mixed into one roll and an optical track made. This optical track would then have to be printed on the finished print for sound.

SUNSET CARSON FILMOGRAPHY

CALL OF THE ROCKIES (1944 - 56 minutes)
Director: Lesley Selander
Filmed: Iverson's
Tagline: *LUSTY ACTION and ROARIN' LAUGHS...with your favorite Western wildcats...SMILEY...and SUNSET...to the tune of spittin' six-guns and the rhythm of galloping hoofs!*
Cast: Smiley Burnette, Sonny "Sunset" Carson, Harry Woods, Kirk Alyn, Ellen Hall, Frank Jaquet, Charles Williams, Jack Kirk, Tom London, Bob Kortman, Edmund Cobb, Bill Nestell, Robert J. Wilke, Brandon Beach, Ralph Bucko, Roy Bucko, Bob Burns, Horace B. Carpenter, Tommy Coats, Franklyn Farnum, Bud Geary, Kit Guard, Herman Hack, Nolan Leary, Rex Lease, Frank McCarroll, Kansas Moehring, Jack O'Shea, Post Park, Carl Sepulveda, Harry Wilson.
Stunts: Henry Wills, Tex Terry, Carol Henry, Cliff Lyons, Fred Graham.

BORDERTOWN TRAIL (1944 - 56 minutes)
Director: Lesley Selander
Filmed: Iverson's
Tagline: *A TWO-FISTED TORNADO...Sunset Carson...trapping sly smugglers...in a thrilling battle of six-guns...and guts! Trigger-Wise Gunmen Save Smuggled Gold In An Exciting, Thrill-Packed Chase!*

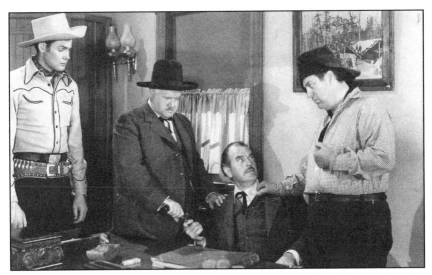

Underhanded physician Frank Jaquet restrains cohort Harry Woods from plugging both partners Smiley Burnette (right) and Sunset Carson (left) in CALL OF THE ROCKIES (Republic, 1944).

Sunset Carson Hollywood Nostalgia Theater promotion. Players included in photo are Jack Kirk and Hank Bell (at top between Sunset photos) plus Ken Terrell (bottom).

Cast: Smiley Burnette, Sunset Carson, Ellen Lowe, Weldon Heyburn, Addison Richards, Francis McDonald, Jack Luden, Rex Lease, John James, Jack Kirk, Henry Wills, Cliff Parkinson, Rusty Cecil, Roy Darmour, Earl Robbins, Chick Hannon, Neal Hart, Jack O'Shea, Ted Wells, Gayne Whitman (Jack Luden's voice), Robert J. Wilke, Post Park.

Stunts: Henry Wills.

CODE OF THE PRAIRIE (1944 - 56 minutes)

Director: Spencer Gordon Bennet

Filmed: Iverson's

Cast: Smiley Burnette, Sunset Carson, Peggy Stewart, Weldon Heyburn, Tom Chatterton, Roy Barcroft, Bud Geary, Tom London, Jack Kirk, Tom Steele, Hank Bell, Horace B. Carpenter, Frank Ellis, Karl Hackett, Herman Hack, Charles King, Nolan Leary, Rex Lease, Jack O'Shea, Robert J. Wilke, Henry Wills, Nellie Walker, Frederick Howard, Ken Terrell.

Stunts: Henry Wills, Post Park, Ken Terrell, Bud Wolfe.

FIREBRANDS OF ARIZONA (1944 - 55 minutes)

Director: Lesley Selander

Filmed: Iverson's and Corriganville

Tagline: *A TIMID SOUL Becomes A Western TERROR! Action with a sock!*

Cast: Smiley Burnette, Sunset Carson, Peggy Stewart, Earle Hodgins, Roy Barcroft, LeRoy Mason, Tom London, Jack Kirk, Bud Geary, Rex Lease, Charles Morton, Hank Bell, Buster Brodie, Bob Burns, Budd Buster, Roy Butler, Horace B. Carpenter, Jess Caven, Victor Cox, Grace Cunard, Dickie Dillion, Maxine Doyle, Phil Dunham, Frank Ellis, Pierce Lyden, Frank McCarroll, Bill Nestell, Frank O'Connor, George Bell, John Cason, Kansas Moehring, Jack O'Shea, Pascale Perry, Tex Terry, Fred "Snowflake" Toones, Robert J. Wilke, Bob Woodward.

Stunts: Bud Geary, Charles Morton, Tom Steele, Bob Woodward, Dale Van Sickel, Joe Yrigoyen, Fred Graham.

Both cowboy Sunset Carson and player Weldon Heyburn are ready to throw pokes at nasty bad guy Ken Terrell in CODE OF THE PRAIRIE (Republic, 1944). Partially hidden behind Heyburn are leading lady Peggy Stewart and old-timer Tom Chatterton. The young bit player just to Sunset's right is Carey Loftin, who would be star George C. Scott's enlisted U.S. Army sergeant jeep driver 26 years later in PATTON (20th Century-Fox, 1970).

SHERIFF OF CIMARRON (1945 - 56 minutes)

Director: Yakima Canutt
Filmed: Iverson's
Cast: Sunset Carson, Linda Stirling, Olin Howlin, Riley Hill, Jack Ingram, Tom London, Jack Kirk, Robert J. Wilke, Jack O'Shea, Ed Cassidy, George Chesebro, Sylvia Arslan, Dickie Dillon, Ralph Bucko, Roy Bucko, Bob Burns, Horace B. Carpenter, Tommy Coats, Tex Cooper, Herman Hack, Carol Henry, Reed Howes, Post Park, Rose Plummer, Hal Price, Gertrude Short, George Sowards, Henry Wills, Cliff Parkinson, Matty Roubert, George Bell, Jack Sparks.
Stunts: Carol Henry, Post Park, Duke Taylor, Henry Wills.

SANTA FE SADDLEMATES (1945 - 58 minutes)

Director: Thomas Carr
Filmed: Iverson's
Cast: Sunset Carson, Linda Stirling, Olin Howlin, Roy Barcroft, Bud Geary, Kenne Duncan, George Chesebro, Robert J. Wilke, Henry Wills, Forbes Murray, Frank Jaquet, Johnny Carpenter, Rex Lease, Horace B. Carpenter, Edmund Cobb, Fred Graham, Chick Hannon, Neal Hart, Carol Henry, Nolan Leary, George Magrill, Kansas Moehring, Bill Nestell, Frank O'Connor, Jack O'Shea, Rose Plummer, Bob Reeves, Duke Taylor, Billy Vincent, Bill Wolfe, Ralph Bucko, Tommy Coats, William Desmond, Phil Keifer.
Stunts: Fred Graham, Carol Henry, Ben Johnson, Duke Taylor, George Magrill, Tom Steele, Post Park, Bill Wolfe.

OREGON TRAIL (1945 - 55 minutes)

Director: Thomas Carr
Filmed: Iverson's
Tagline: *Flaming guns and flashing fists in story that starts at a trot and ends in a gallop!*
Cast: Sunset Carson, Peggy Stewart, Frank Jaquet, Mary Carr, John Merton, Si Jenks, Bud Geary, Kenne Duncan, Steve Winston, Lee Shumway, Earle Hodgins, Tom London, Horace B. Carpenter, Martha Carroll, Tommy Coats, Monte Hale, Rex Lease, Cactus Mack, George Magrill, Bud Osborne, Jamesson Shade, Sheila Stuart, Tex Terry, Henry

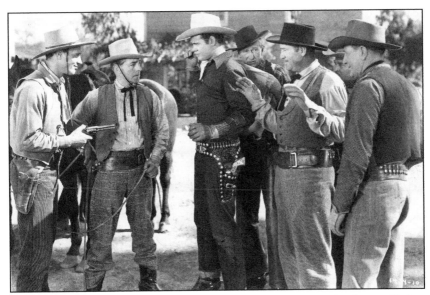

It looks like curtains for lawman Sunset Carson as badman Bob Wilke (with pistol) and pal Kenne Duncan detain our hero in SANTA FE SADDLEMATES (Republic, 1945). Olin Howlin, Roy Barcroft, Bill Wolfe and Bud Geary watch.

Imprisoned rancher George Chesebro and special investigator Sunset Carson learn the secret, via saddle pommels, of how jewel smugglers are transporting their contraband between the United States and Mexico in SANTA FE SADDLEMATES (Republic, 1945).

Wills, Pascale Perry, Jess Caven, Billy Dix, Frank O'Connor, Tommy Coats, Hank Bell, Roy Bucko, Henry Wills, Carol Henry.

Stunts: Tom Steele, Henry Wills, Carol Henry.

BANDITS OF THE BADLANDS (1945 - 55 minutes)

Director: Thomas Carr

Filmed: Iverson's

Tagline: *EXTRA!!! RANGER TURNS BANDIT...but only until he finds the badlands bandits who murdered his brother! ACTION SPEAKS LOUDER THAN WORDS — and this lad gives you action with a bang!*

Cast: Sunset Carson, Peggy Stewart, Si Jenks, John Merton, Forrest Taylor, Wade Crosby, Jack Ingram, Monte Hale, Fred Graham, Alan Ward, Robert J. Wilke, Tex Terry, Jack O'Shea, Melva Ainstead, Ralph Bucko, Roy Bucko, Foxy Callahan, Horace B. Carpenter, Tommy Coats, Augie Gomez, Herman Hack, Jack Kirk, Bert LeBaron, Frank McCarroll, Post Park, Pascale Perry, Marshall Reed, Bob Reeves, Carl Sepulveda, Charles Stevens, Brick Sullivan, Charles Sullivan, Herman Willingham, Henry Wills, Bob Woodward, Billy Dix, Cactus Mack, Frank O'Connor, Artie Ortego, George Bell, William Duncan.

Stunts: Duke Taylor, Bob Woodward, Bud Geary, Henry Wills, Fred Graham, Chuck Roberson.

ROUGH RIDERS OF CHEYENNE (1945 - 56 minutes)

Director: Thomas Carr

Filmed: Iverson's

Cast: Sunset Carson, Peggy Stewart, Mira McKinney, Monte Hale, Wade Crosby, Michael Sloane, Kenne Duncan, Tom London, Eddy Waller, Robert J. Wilke, Tex Terry, Jack Rockwell, Hank Bell, Roy Bucko, Harriette Haddon, Rex Lease, Jack Luden, Cactus Mack, Carl Mathews, Artie Ortego, Beverly Reedy, Henry Wills, Jack O'Shea, Ralph Bucko, Jess Caven, George Bell, Nellie Walker, Kansas Moehring.

Stunts: Bobbie Dorree, Tom Steele, Henry Wills, Cliff Lyons, Carol Henry.

Severely shot Jack Kirk is comforted with support from Tex Terry, Alan Ward, Marshall Reed, Frank O'Connor, unknown player, Sunset Carson, and Jack O'Shea in BANDITS OF THE BADLANDS (Republic, 1945). Sunset is after brother Monte Hale's killer.

The grim face on ranch foreman Monte Hale signals he isn't ready to sing cowboy tunes while aiming a gun directly at land inheritor Sunset Carson for ROUGH RIDERS OF CHEYENNE (Republic, 1945).

THE CHEROKEE FLASH (1945 - 55 minutes)

Director: Thomas Carr

Filmed: Iverson's

Cast: Sunset Carson, Linda Stirling, Tom London, Roy Barcroft, John Merton, Bud Geary, Frank Jaquet, Fred Graham, Joe McGuinn, Pierce Lyden, James Linn, Bud Osborne, Edmund Cobb, Hank Bell, Roy Bucko, Ralph Bucko, George Chesebro, Herman Hack, Tommy Coats, Chick Hannon, Marian Kerrigan, Cactus Mack, George Sowards, Bill Wolfe, Jess Caven, George Bell, Frank O'Connor, Neal Hart, Kansas Moehring.

Stunts: Duke Green, Fred Graham, Tom Steele, Ken Terrell.

DAYS OF BUFFALO BILL (1946 - 56 minutes)

Director: Thomas Carr

Filmed: Iverson's

Tagline: *Dire BLAZING ADVENTURE... With Your New Hero of the Plains!*

Cast: Sunset Carson, Peggy Stewart, Tom London, James Craven, Rex Lease, Edmund Cobb, Eddie Parker, Michael Sloane, Jay Kirby, George Chesebro, Ed Cassidy, Frank O'Connor, Roy Bucko, Foxy Callahan, Jess Caven, Tommy Coats, Tex Cooper, Frank Ellis, Kit Guard, Lew Morphy, Cliff Parkinson, Pascale Perry, Jose Pulido, Nick Thompson, Jack Tornek, George Bell, Kansas Moehring, Jack O'Shea, John Carpenter.

Stunts: Eddie Parker, Tom Steele, Dale Van Sickel.

ALIAS BILLY THE KID (1946 - 56 minutes)

Director: Thomas Carr

Filmed: Iverson's

Cast: Sunset Carson, Peggy Stewart, Tom London, Roy Barcroft, Russ Whiteman, Tom Chatterton, Tex Terry, Pierce Lyden, James R. Linn, Stanley Price, Edward Cassidy, Jack O'Shea, Jack Kirk, Jack Rockwell, George Bell, George Sowards, Riley Hill (Russ Whiteman double at Iverson's).

Stunts: Tom Steele, Cliff Lyons, Post Park.

THE EL PASO KID (1946 - 54 minutes)
Director: Thomas Carr
Filmed: Iverson's
Cast: Sunset Carson, Marie Harmon, Hank Patterson, Edmund Cobb, Robert Filmer, Wheaton Chambers, Zon Murray, Tex Terry, Ed Cassidy, Johnny Carpenter, Post Park, Charles Sullivan, Jack Sparks, Art Dillard, Phil Keifer, Roy Bucko, Chuck Roberson.
Stunts: Johnny Carpenter, Fred Carson, Tom Steele, Chuck Roberson.

RED RIVER RENEGADES (1946 - 55 minutes)
Director: Thomas Carr
Filmed: Iverson's
Taglines: *Action! Action! ACTION!...as fightin' son of the West solves mystery of vanishing stagecoaches!*
SUNSET CARSON FRONTS FOR UNCLE SAM… and the mail goes through!
IT'S CURTAINS FOR THE ROAD AGENTS WHEN CARSON COMES TO TOWN … Action all the way when Uncle Sam pins a badge on Sunny!
Cast: Sunset Carson, Peggy Stewart, Tom London, Ted Adams, LeRoy Mason, Kenne Duncan, Bruce Langley, Edmund Cobb, Bob Burns, Budd Buster, Fred Graham, Herman Hack, Cactus Mack, Kansas Moehring, Lew Morphy, Stanley Price, Jack Rockwell, Carl Sepulveda, Duke Taylor, Tex Terry, Jack Torek, Charles Williams, George Bell, Jess Caven, Jack Montgomery, Cliff Lyons, George Sowards.
Stunts: Fred Graham, Cliff Lyons, Duke Taylor, Tom Steele, Dale Van Sickel.

RIO GRANDE RAIDERS (1946 - 56 minutes)
Director: Thomas Carr
Filmed: Iverson's
Tagline: *VENGEANCE Beyond the RIO GRANDE!*
Cast: Sunset Carson, Linda Stirling, Bob Steele, Tom London, Tristram Coffin, Edmund Cobb, Jack O'Shea, Tex Terry, Kenne Duncan, Roy Bucko, Bob Burns, Fred Burns, Herman Hack, LeRoy Mason (narrator), Frank O'Connor, Harry

Stagecoach driver Post Park holds horse reins as outlaw Sunset Carson and female lead Marie Harmon tend to wounded Hank Patterson in THE EL PASO KID (Republic, 1946).

Cattle herders Tom London and Sunset Carson prepare to confront troublemaker Eddie Parker during DAYS OF BUFFALO BILL (Republic, 1946). Watching in the background are bearded Tex Cooper and young actor Michael Sloane.

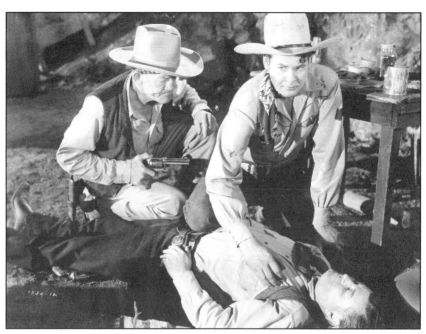

A concerned Sunset Carson feels the heart of gambler Rex Lease, inadvertently shot by Carson pal Tom London before questioning in DAYS OF BUFFALO BILL (Republic, 1946).

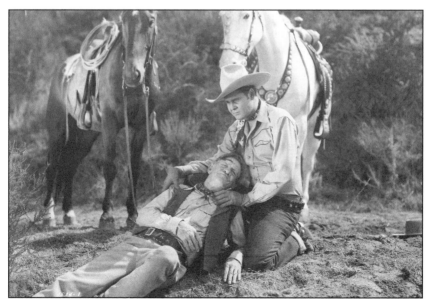

Badly injured Tom London is looked after on the trail by saddlemate Sunset Carson during DAYS OF BUFFALO BILL (Republic, 1946).

Ranch owner Peggy Stewart is determined to gun down newly-hired foreman Sunset Carson whom she strongly accuses of murdering her brother in earlier scenes from DAYS OF BUFFALO BILL (Republic, 1946). Peggy eventually wounds Sunset.

Strang, Al Taylor, Blackie Whiteford, Bobby Barber, Jack Kirk (hidden shotgun man).
Stunts: Tom Steele, Joe Yrigoyen.

SUNSET CARSON RIDES AGAIN (1947 - 63 minutes) [Color]

Tagline: *Rough, Tough Action!*
Director: Oliver Drake
Filmed: Oliver Drake Ranch
Cast: Sunset Carson, Al Terry, Pat Starling, Dan White, Pat Gleason, John L. Cason, Stephen Keyes, Ron Ormond, Bob Curtis, Joe Hiser, Bill Vall, Forrest Matthews, Don Gray, Dale Harrison (Sunset's brother), The Rodeo Revelers.

FIGHTING MUSTANG (1948 - 56 minutes) [Color]

Director: Oliver Drake
Filmed: Oliver Drake Ranch and Pear Blossom
Cast: Sunset Carson, Al Terry, Pat Starling, Felice Richmond, Polly McKay, William Val, Forrest Matthews, Lee Roberts, Bob Curtis, Stephen Keyes, Tex Wilson, Al Ferguson, Hugh Hooker, Dale Harrison (Sunset's brother), Little Joe's Wranglers (music), Ralph Bucko, Don Gray, Joe Hiser.

DEADLINE (1948 - 57 minutes) [Color]

Director: Oliver Drake
Filmed: Oliver Drake Ranch and Pear Blossom
Taglines: *GUNNIN' FOR TROUBLE with FORTY-FIVES or FISTS!*
SUNSET CARSON and his horse CACTUS Jr. Ride again!
HIS TRIGGER-FINGER ON EVERY OUTLAW IN THE WEST!
FORTY-FIVES or FISTS! He was at his best when the West was at its worst!
Cast: Sunset Carson, Al Terry, Pat Starling, Pat Gleason, Lee Roberts, Stephen Keyes, Frank Ellis, Forrest Matthews, Bob Curtis, Phil Arnold, Joe Hiser, Donald Gray, Buck Monroe, Al Wyatt, Sr.
Stunts: Boyd Stockman, Al Wyatt, Sr.

RIO GRANDE (1949 - 56 minutes)
Director: Norman Sheldon
Filmed: Juanita, Texas
Cast: Sunset Carson, Evohn Keyes, Lee Morgan, Bobby Deats, Henry Garcia, Bobby Clack (aka Bobby Clark), Maria Louisa Marulanda, Curley Rucker, Don Gray, Houston Teehee, Frank Lawyer, Carmen Grasso, Neil Levang, Walter Clambake Jr.

BATTLING MARSHAL (1950 - 55 minutes) [Color]
Director: Oliver Drake
Filmed: Oliver Drake Ranch
Cast: Sunset Carson, Al Terr, Pat Starling, Lee Roberts, Richard Bartell, Jack Baxley, Buck Buckley, Alfred Caldwell, Dale Carson (Sunset's brother — he is now billing himself as Carson instead of Harrison), Bob Curtis, Eddie Elwood, Pat Gleason, Donald Gray, Joe Hiser, Stephen Keyes, Forrest Matthews, William Val.

MARSHAL OF WINDY HOLLOW (1972)
Director: Jerry Whittington
Filmed: Windy Hollow, Kentucky (near Owensboro)
(Although Tex Ritter and Ken Maynard had small roles, most of the rest of the cast are relatively unknowns.)
Synopsis: The Marshal (Sunset Carson) calls in the head of the Texas Rangers (Ken Maynard) to help track down the disappearance of an entire wagon train. Maynard discovers the outlaws were robbing the settlers, stealing the gold, and dumping the wagons with the settlers into the Canyon River. The Rangers then trap the outlaws in the canyon. Some of the outlaws get blown up in their hideout, while the others are arrested by Marshal Carson and brought to the town of Windy Hollow for trial.

(All filming locations listed above are for Sunset's starring films, and are in California unless otherwise specified).

THE NON-STARRING FILMS

STAGE DOOR CANTEEN (United Artists, 1943 - 132 minutes)
Director: Frank Borzage
Filmed: Fox Movietone Studio in New York City and RKO Pathe Studios in Los Angeles
Cast: Cheryl Walker, William Terry, Marjorie Riordan, Lon McCallister, Margaret Early, Michael Harrison (Sunset Carson), Dorothea Kent, Fred Brady, Peggy Lee, Lina Romay, Sully Mason, Harry Babbitt, Julie Conway, Trudy Irwin, Jack Max, Helene Dumas, Dorothy Fields, Arlene Francis, Virginia Kaye, Marion Moore, Elizabeth Morgan, plus extra players Judith Anderson, Kenny Baker, Tallulah Bankhead, Ralph Bellamy, Edgar Bergen, Charlie McCarthy, Ray Bolger, Ina Claire, Katharine Cornell, Gracie Fields, Lynn Fontaine, Helen Hayes, Katharine Hepburn, Hugh Herbert, Jean Hersholt, George Jessel, Gypsy Rose Lee, Alfred Lunt, Harpo Marx, Elsa Maxwell, Yehudi Menuhin, Ethel Merman, Paul Muni, Merle Oberon, George Raft, Lanny Ross, Martha Scott, Ethel Waters, Johnny Weissmuller, Ed Wynn, Henry Armetta, Benny Baker, Helen Broderick, Lloyd Corrigan, Jane Darwell, William Demarest, Virginia Field, Vinton Freedley, Ann Gillis, Lucille Gleason, Vera Gordon, Virginia Grey, Sam Jaffe, Allen Jenkins, Roscoe Karns, Tom Kennedy, Otto Kruger, June Lang, Betty Lawford, Bert Lytell, Aline MacMahon, Horace MacMahon, Helen Menken, Peggy Moran, Ralph Morgan, Alan Mowbray, Elliott Nugent, Patrick O'Moore, Franklin Pangborn, Helen Parrish, Brock Pemberton, Selena Royle, Marion Shockley, Cornelia Otis Skinner, Ned Sparks, Bill Stern, Arleen Whelan, Dame May Whitty and the famous bands of Count Basie, Xavier Cugat, Benny Goodman, Kay Kyser, Guy Lombardo, Freddy Martin.

JANIE (Warner Bros., 1944 - 100 minutes)
Director: Michael Curtiz
Filmed: Lake Malibu and Warner Bros. Studios
Cast: Joyce Reynolds, Robert Hutton, Edward Arnold, Ann

Harding, Alan Hale, Robert Benchley, Clare Foley, Barbara Brown, Hattie McDaniel, Dick Erdman, Jackie Moran, Ann Gillis, Ruth Tobey, Virginia Patton, Colleen Townsend, William Frambes, Georgia Lee Settle, Peter Stackpole, Michael Harrison (Sunset Carson), Russell Hicks.

BELLS OF ROSARITA (Republic, 1945 - 68 minutes)
Director: Frank McDonald
Filmed: Iverson's and Republic Studios
Cast: Roy Rogers, Trigger (horse), George "Gabby" Hayes, Dale Evans, Adele Mara, Grant Withers, Addison Richards, Roy Barcroft, Janet Martin, Robert Mitchell Boychoir, Bob Nolan and The Sons of the Pioneers, Republic guest stars Wild Bill Elliott, Allan Lane, Donald Barry, Robert Livingston, and Sunset Carson, plus Charles Sullivan, Kenne Duncan, Edward Cassidy, Forbes Murray, Paul Power, Billy Cartledge, Cactus Mack, Eddie Kane, Tom London, Roger Creed, Mary McCarty, Marian Kerrigan, Rosamond James, Billy Cummings, Sam Ash, Larry Williams, Irving Fulton, Poodles Hanneford, Tom Plank, Buster Brodie, Carl Leviness, Jesse Graves, Hank Bell, Syd Saylor, Craig Lawrence, Robert J. Wilke, Rex Lease, Earle Hodgins, George Barton, Marin Sais, Helen Talbot, Barbara Elliott, Wally West, Dale Van Sickel, Frank McCarroll.
Stunts: Joe Yrigoyen, Dale Van Sickel, Frank McCarroll, Gil Perkins, Duke Green, Duke Taylor, Harvey Parry.

SEABO (1978) [aka BUCKSTONE COUNTY PRISON]
Starring Earl Owensby, Don Barry, and country singer David Allan Coe.

ALIEN OUTLAW (1985)
Starring Stephen Winegard. Lash LaRue also had a part in the film.

SIMON AND SIMON TV episode — "Down-Home Country Blues" (1985).

SUNSET'S WESTERN TROUBLEMAKERS

Republic bad guy Bob Wilke's eight B-Western roles with Sunset Carson in 1944 and 1945 were very small with the exception of SHERIFF OF CIMARRON (Republic, 1945). Bob then became extraordinarily active on the Charles Starrett movies (Columbia, 1945-52) plus Tim Holt's RKO sagas (1951-52). After doing Gary Cooper's famous A-hayburner HIGH NOON (United Artists, 1952) as one of the main outlaws, Wilke was to gain greater movie traction once the 1950s progressed on prominent big-budgeters like THE FAR COUNTRY (Universal, 1955), THE LONE RANGER (Warner Bros., 1956), and MAN OF THE WEST (United Artists, 1958).

With his ever-present authoritative voice in the 1940s, Republic out-law Kenne Duncan was extremely busy hounding every studio cow-boy (Don "Red" Barry, Wild Bill Elliott, Roy Rogers, Allan Lane, etc.) in 61 B-Westerns, including Sunset Carson whom he had the gall to back-shoot in OREGON TRAIL (Republic, 1945). Kenne did more skunk duties at Monogram and Columbia into the early 1950s on the low-budgeters of Johnny Mack Brown, Jimmy Wakely, Whip Wilson, and Gene Autry.

The always mean John Cason did only a walk-on with Sunset Carson's FIREBRANDS OF ARIZONA (Republic, 1944), but later joined the B-cowboy star in a meaty crooked ranch partner role for SUNSET CARSON RIDES AGAIN (Yucca, 1947). Besides mid-1940s PRC screen villainy with cowboy lead Buster Crabbe, Cason also connected to Republic and Columbia badman B-parts on Allan "Rocky" Lane, Rex Allen, Charles Starrett, and Gene Autry films, plus the low-budgeters of Lash LaRue and Jimmy Ellison well into the 1950s. Nastiness was John's trademark.

Forever blunt with any villainy against anybody on-screen at Republic, Bud Geary did 57 B-Westerns there through the mid-1940s, one in which he severely beat up elderly Tom London as a crooked sheriff in THE CHEROKEE FLASH (Republic, 1945) with Sunset Carson. Other Republic horse-opera stars on whose features Geary worked were Wild Bill Elliott, Bob Livingston, Allan Lane, and Don "Red" Barry. Bud lost his life in a fatal car acident after finishing MAN FROM RAINBOW VALLEY (Republic, 1946) that starred cowboy singer Monte Hale.

Menace seemed always in Lee Roberts' voice, whether playing bad or good guys in B-Westerns. Lee began at PRC and Monogram during the 1940s, eventually making his way to Sunset Carson's DEADLINE (Yucca, 1948). Lee later returned basically to Monogram by 1950 for more low-budget oaters with Whip Wilson and Johnny Mack Brown until mid-1952, then grabbed the great Indian agent role in THE LONE RANGER (Warner Bros., 1956) where he strongly challenged tribe hater Lyle Bettger.

Ugly-faced Bob Kortman made his way into the 1930s Columbia B-Westerns of Buck Jones and Tim McCoy. Kortman then emoted on 16 Republic low-budget oaters to early 1944. One of his best was John Wayne's WINDS OF THE WASTELAND (Republic, 1936) where he razzed / fought the star. Bob also latched onto mischief character parts with eight of B-action cowboy Don "Red" Barry's 1942-43 movies. He was full of skulduggery for Sunset Carson's CALL OF THE ROCKIES (Republic, 1944). About this same time, Kortman ended his prolific sagebrusher career finishing up on Columbia and PRC horse operas of Charles Starrett and Buster Crabbe by the mid-1940s.

Harry Woods possessed a snarling face with his mustache and gravel voice — perfect evils he used to menace numerous B-Western heroes from 1930 to 1950 at Columbia, Monogram, Universal, Republic, and RKO. Harry really growled at Sunset Carson in CALL OF THE ROCKIES (Republic, 1944) as a crooked mining-goods supplier.

A DIFFERENT PERSPECTIVE

by Richard B. Smith III

(After completing my research, I asked noted Western film historian Richard B. Smith III to submit his thoughts on Sunset and his films. Obviously, there will be some repetition, but I believe the reader will enjoy Smith's views.)

Sunset's Meteoric Rise/Fall at Republic

Oklahoma and Texas rodeo cowboy star Winifred Maurice Harrison had corralled only limited Hollywood acting experience with portrayals of U.S. Army enlistees in STAGE DOOR CANTEEN (United Artists, 1943) and JANIE (Warner Bros., 1944). But better movie days were ahead for this 6-4 (or 6-6, depending whom one believes) film neophyte with his appealing drawl, bright smile, and flirtatious manner with the opposite sex.

Republic comedian Smiley Burnette, workhorse since early July 1935 for this popular movie studio as sidekick in B-Westerns of stars Gene Autry, Roy Rogers, Eddie Dew and Bob Livingston, had finished filming his latest low-budget sagebrusher with Livingston, THE LARAMIE TRAIL (Republic, 1944) on Christmas Eve 1943.

THE LARAMIE TRAIL would turn out to be Bob Livingston's 32nd and concluding lead role as a Republic movie cowboy since 1936 that also included 29 starring B-Westerns as Stony Brooke (1936-38, 1939-41) in the studio's *The Three Mesquiteers* series. He had also lensed seven B-Westerns for the minor Producers Releasing Corporation (PRC) from mid-October 1942 through late July 1943. With Livingston suddenly out of Republic low-budget Westerns and cast into the studio's modest-costing dramas by end of January 1944, Republic began plans for a new series of B-horse opera entries. They placed Smiley Burnette with the recently signed Michael Harrison (a name he had used for some time) to star in the studio's fresh *Superior Westerns* series. The Michael Harrison name was soon changed to Sonny "Sunset" Carson by President Herbert J. Yates.

How Carson became connected to Republic as Livingston's chosen successor has never been thoroughly revealed, but he pacted a term contract of $150 per week on March 18, 1944, the day the initial Burnette/Carson, CALL OF THE ROCKIES (Republic, 1944), commenced before cameras.

First plans were for Smiley and Sunset to make eight B-Westerns. Burnette would still retain his long-identified Frog Millhouse character, but Carson was to exclusively portray himself with the Sonny part of his name abandoned by Republic after CALL OF THE ROCKIES.

Sunset began wearing two stag-handled, nickel-plated pistols in holsters with the gun butts forward similar to B-cowboy lead Wild Bill Elliott, then also commencing production for Republic's new *Red Ryder* series.

The fan mail for Sunset Carson coming to the studio was heavy as Smiley Burnette became so dissatisfied with staying at Republic that he decided, possibly because of unsatisfactory salary arrangements, not to sign a new term contract after completing a 4th role with Carson in FIREBRANDS OF ARIZONA (Republic, 1944) by June 30, 1944. These B-

Westerns cost $45,000 - $50,000 each to make.

After Burnette's departure from Republic, Carson was to remain camera idle and dusting off his boots for over five months until December 5, 1944, when the studio elevated him to permanent solo status starting on the Yakima Canutt-directed SHERIFF OF CIMARRON (Republic, 1945). On December 14, the last day of shooting, Sunset broke one of his wrists, but was able to finish acting before checking into a Hollywood hospital for treatment. Sunset's two guns were now butts backward.

The first inkling of Sunset's imbibing too much alcohol can be seen with him as one of Republic's B-cowboy movie guest stars on Roy Rogers' $220,000 costing BELLS OF ROSARITA (Republic, 1945). Carson's initial footage here is on Republic's Western Street where he stages a fight-shootout confrontation with bad guys Dale Van Sickel and Frank McCarroll. Sunset's eyes appear very blood shot as if he has experienced a prior night of heavy drinking.

Sunset's liking of the bottle was to soon spur more personal warnings from Republic President Herbert Yates; however, by the time Carson went into action scenes March 24, 1945 for OREGON TRAIL (Republic, 1945), his 3rd solo Republic B-Western, he had received a weekly salary raise to $200.

Carson kept doing more horse operas throughout 1945 at a relatively steady pace. In between doing B-Westerns, Sunset visited the Republic movie set of actress Jane Withers, who was making AFFAIRS OF GERALDINE (Republic, 1946) as filming was done in January 1946.

By the time he went into RED RIVER RENEGADES (Republic, 1946), on March 19, 1946, Sunset's weekly pay had been bumped to $250. After finishing shots on his 10th B-oater March 27, Carson's perils with Yates were to take a sudden and dramatic turn several months later.

Republic Pictures, for quite some time, had established and promoted what it termed a "good neighbor policy" with Mexico by having the company's film product in that country's movie theaters during the 1940s. This was not only an important endeavor for Yates to receive extra coin from outside countries such as Mexico but for other big Hollywood film corporations as well.

Probably sometime in late Spring 1946, to further enhance Republic playdates with Mexico, Yates had all his B-film cowboy stars visit the country for a social reception hosted by the President of Mexico.

Sunset Carson was with his fellow horse saddlers, but attended this reception, possibly held in the Mexican capital of Mexico City, quite inebriated and in the company of an underage girl. Word of this unfortunate incident filtered back to Yates who decided enough was enough with Carson's drinking bouts. Once Sunset made his way back to Republic, Yates terminated his term-player contract with the provision that the movie cowboy could lense RIO GRANDE RAIDERS (Republic, 1946), already scheduled for production, and then permanently exit the Republic lot. Yates reportedly vowed Carson would do no other movie work in Hollywood if he had his way.

Carson temporarily went into a new Republic film season for 1946-47 with RIO GRANDE RAIDERS on July 8, 1946. The studio earlier had published a fancy exploitation brochure titled "Sunset Carson Sets the Pace In Six-Gun Action." That advertised eight more scheduled sagebrush features Sunset was to have made if Yates hadn't sacked him. Whether RIO GRANDE RAIDERS was one of these titles under another name in the brochure could not be determined.

In the late author Jack Mathis' *Republic Confidential* (Volume 2 — The Players), published in 1992, Carson's Republic contract ended on July 15, 1946, the same day RIO GRANDE RAIDERS wound up camera shots. The last 11 Sunset acted in had production costs of $36,000 - $46,000 each. Ten of them had been directed by Thomas Carr.

While this 11th and end solo Sunset Republic B-Western was being produced, *Life* magazine sent photographers to the Republic back lot to snap a series of pictures of actors, technicians, and some of the tricks used in making a low-budget Western of that time. This photo spread of seven pages appeared in *Life*'s October 7, 1946 edition.

Probably by March or April 1947 and partially defying Herbert Yates' edict that he wouldn't find new acting work after Republic, Sunset hooked up with producer Walt Mattox of Yucca Pictures, a small movie outfit, to film new B-Westerns as their star. They were to be directed by Oliver Drake. But Sunset was finding himself shortchanged with this new venture. These features, as it turns out, would be shot for just several thousand each — probably in the neighborhood of $5,000 — and shot in 16mm color, but blown up to 35mm for what turned out to be a limited theatrical release. Carson's pay for doing these four with Mattox for distribution through Astor Pictures was undoubtedly very little.

After concluding only the four movies lensed with Walt Mattox, probably by late 1947, Sunset hooked up with the even cheaper Lautem Productions outfit, maybe in 1948 or 1949, to emote for the B-Western RIO GRANDE (Lautem, 1949), a true disaster for the B-Western genre, also released through Astor.

This was the end for Sunset Carson. He would never do any more movie Westerns that were actually released, instead confining the remainder of his active life to rodeos, personal appearances, and later film festivals in the 1970s and 1980s.

THE B-WESTERNS OF SUNSET CARSON

(Note: Reviews of Sunset's first four films in 1944 with Republic — CALL OF THE ROCKIES, BORDERTOWN TRAIL, CODE OF THE PRAIRIE, and FIREBRANDS OF ARIZONA — can be found within Smiley Burnette's B-Western filmography.)

SHERIFF OF CIMARRON (Republic, 1945). For his 1st solo starring B-Western, Sunset Carson was placed with excellent action director Yakima Canutt, who thrust the new studio movie cowboy amid a gang of holdup artists and murderers with Bennett Cohen's script. Carson is an ex-jailbird just released from prison after three years, having been falsely convicted of cattle rustling, but Sunset has no idea yet that skunk brother Riley Hill, a gang member was responsible for the frame-up. After foiling an attempted express office robbery attempt for a gold-filled strongbox, the cowboy is named Cimarron's new sheriff. In dynamic fashion, Sunset gradually whittles down the gunmen with straight shooting. Hill then murders shipment head Jack Kirk in another failed try. Gang leader Jack Ingram poses as a fake U. S. Marshal which enables him and Hill to finally plunder the gold from Kirk daughter Linda Stirling. Sunset sees through the ruse and fatally guns Ingram, and then knocks out Hill during an exciting cave fight. Character player Olin Howlin, as a physician, partially sidekicks with Carson who bullwhips badman Henry Wills off his horse in an earlier scene. This feature was a great B-Western action start for Sunset at Republic which never billed Carson horse Silver in the credits.

BELLS OF ROSARITA (Republic, 1945). Before resuming his own low-budget sagebrushers in early February 1945, Carson was cast as one of the studio's five present and past B-Western cowboy leads along with Wild Bill Elliott, Allan Lane, Donald Barry, and Robert Livingston for this expensive Roy Rogers musical horse opera which Republic greatly ballyhooed as part of its 10th anniversary celebration in 1945. The routine plot has leading lady Dale Evans' ranch/circus greatly threatened with foreclosure by sneak realtor Grant Withers unless Evans can raise $6,400 to pay the balance owed, which her late father had already done 11 years earlier with a signed receipt from Withers. Sunset and the other movie cowboys go after Withers and his ruffians in pulsating, rhythmic horseback footage with excellent Joseph Dubin scoring once this receipt has been stolen from a bank vault. The owlhoots are captured one by one as Carson bullwhips a pistol from badman Duke Taylor's hand while astride horse Silver, then knocks him out. Sunset is last among the movie guest cowboys billed on screen, but introduced first before the circus crowd just prior to this oatuner's fadeout. An energetic and excellent Republic offering.

SANTA FE SADDLEMATES (Republic, 1945). A new director and also for the remainder of Sunset's Republic prairie adventures, Thomas Carr, really lets Carson have an exciting and fighting time here — a total of six slugfests, two prolonged and four short. New Mexico is plagued by jewel smugglers on its boundary with Mexico. As special investigator for state territorial governor Frank Jaquet, Sunset Carson is assigned to break up the border hoppers, naturally headed by the wonderful acting Roy Barcroft. As the town's "leading citizen," Republic's chief cowboy movie villain puts on an amazing dialogue of uncontrollable hysterics for one scene saying: "I tell you, it's an outrage! A defenseless stranger struck down on the main road leading into town in broad daylight, and the murderer gets away scot free. It's enough to make a man's blood boil. Such lawlessness!" This was an example of the beauty of Barcroft's dramatic skills, phonily reacting to his own criminal activities. Sunset is aided in his quest to foil the smugglers by tenderfoot Olin Howlin and reporter/saloon songbird Linda Stirling, who nicely warbles "Oh, Mister!" and "LaCucaracha." Carson winds up Barcroft's smuggling operation via saddle pommels with a rough slugfest against the villain along with a blazing shootout styming the other jewel runners. This was the greatest of Carson's features.

OREGON TRAIL (Republic, 1945). A slick outlaw leader and his assorted robbers have stolen $50,000 in gold bullion from the Union Pacific Railroad and completely vanished. After the looters, in quick gallop, are railroad detectives Sunset Carson and Lee Shumway. The gang has smoothly secreted into the lawless town of Gunsight with big shot John Merton, now a saloon operator. Merton wants to purchase the metropolis from owner Frank Jaquet for a rail shipping center. The latter refuses which leads to his quick demise. Carson has to confront gunmen Kenne Duncan and Bud Geary without much success because of drunken, comic judge Earle Hodgins, in league with Merton. Actual head boss is editor Steve Winston who melted the stolen gold into his printing press. With help from elderly actress Mary Carr and granddaughter Peggy Stewart, Sunset has a fisticuffs showdown with Winston. Another pal of the cowboy here is humorous, bearded Si Jenks, thesping in the George "Gabby" Hayes tradition. Carr, mother of director Thomas Carr, is extremely spry in the part for her years, even firing shorts at gunman Bud Geary who pleads: "Please, Grandma, turn me loose. If the town finds out that you nabbed me, I'll never live it down. Grandma, I'm supposed to be a bad man." Another excellent Carson outing.

BANDITS OF THE BADLANDS (Republic, 1945). Territorial outlaws are plaguing the area. During a cattle rustling raid by gunmen John Merton, Bob Wilke, and Jack Ingram, the latter is mortally wounded by Texas Ranger Sunset Carson. Ingram brother Merton exacts revenge by killing Carson relative Monte Hale, forcing Sunset to temporarily resign as Ranger and take stage driver Si Jenks for needed help to the gang hideout of Kincaid's Hole. This is a tense, very good Carson Western as he attempts infiltration by taking Wilke off a traveling coach into the rundown town. Sunset fights his way into the gang by whipping cohort Fred Graham in a brawl; mainly done in the cellar of a saloon, then he guns down Graham for a shootout. The Rangers finally reach the gang hideout for a blazing exchange of lead. Merton is wounded with Carson taking him to the cave where Hale was killed. Sunset beats the murderer to a pulp, but is prevented from strangling Merton by Jenks and Ranger Captain Alan Ward.

ROUGH RIDERS OF CHEYENNE (Republic, 1945). A fast-paced shooting sagebrusher, it's an old two-family feud involving son Sunset Carson and father Eddy Waller against a neighboring rancher, the hateful Mira McKinney and offspring Peggy Stewart and Michael Sloane. Then there's a chief, unknown antagonist having his gang stir up the ferocious feelings between the two factions so he can grab off rich valley lands for added use as an outlaw hideout. Once Carson's dad is killed by this menacing chief, Sunset gradually works to bring the two families together plus puts the antagonist and his gang out of business with an action-loaded climax. Future Republic B-Western star Monte Hale has a good supporting role as Sunset's ranch foreman, and warbles "The Old Chisholm Trail."

THE CHEROKEE FLASH (Republic, 1945). Here we have a big role reversal with studio badman Roy Barcroft, known by this B-Western's title as a former outlaw trying to stay legit after serving prison time. Only his old gang won't let him. This precarious situation worries adopted son Sunset Carson after gang member Pierce Lyden is knifed dead by underhanded attorney John Merton who wants local ranchers' water rights. Even more troubling circumstances evolve for Carson as foreman pal Tom London is viciously beaten in jail for information on escaped Barcroft's whereabouts by sheriff Bud Geary, secretly in the pay of Merton. But Sunset frightens the gang chief into revealing himself for a thrilling knockdown, knuckle fest at the film's conclusion after Merton fatally stabs Geary. London is a surprisingly good actor without false teeth for the positive, fast-paced dramatics.

DAYS OF BUFFALO BILL (Republic, 1946). What seems like a friendly game of poker for herder Sunset Carson after a cattle drive turns into the nightmare murder of rancher Jay Kirby and Carson's fleeing of the law to prove his innocence. Gamblers James Craven and Rex Lease have found a map noting gold on Kirby's spread. To enrich themselves, the two partners coerce banker Edmund Cobb into attempting foreclosure on the property, now solely owned by the deceased's sister Peggy Stewart who needs to sell her horses to pay off such indebtedness. It's a challenging time for Sunset until he grabs both Craven, actual Kirby murderer, and Lease in the ranch mine cave. It's a good galloper for Sunset Carson who reluctantly takes advice from sidekick Tom London, having hastily wounded Lease with a bullet before Carson could question him.

ALIAS BILLY THE KID (Republic, 1946). Roy Barcroft is in this excellent Sunset Carson sagebrusher as a so-called honest cattle broker and up to no good as usual. Barcroft's taking stock from gullible, local ranchers and selling the herds at high market prices and hogging 90 percent of the profits for himself. Carson is on the trail of whoever fatally plugged a fellow Texas Ranger which leads soon enough to Barcroft who murdered his former business competitor. This makes dead rival daughter Peggy Stewart get even with Barcroft by taking his ill-gotten finances. After Stewart as well, Carson discovers Barcroft's trickery and has a shoot-em-up fight showdown with the thief and his gang of rustlers for final justice.

THE EL PASO KID (Republic, 1946). Gold-dust thieves led by outlaw Robert Filmer almost sucker pals Sunset Carson and Hank Patterson into a life of crime, but Carson, however, has a change of heart after murder is committed during a robbery and when Patterson is shot and wounded in the getaway. Quitting the gang and quelling a stage heist, Sunset is made deputy to Sheriff Edmund Cobb. Carson is then forced by the gang to participate with an express office stickup, but eventually proves his innocence by capturing Filmer during a slugfest that prompts pardon from the state governor. Good Sunset Carson vehicle.

RED RIVER RENEGADES (Republic, 1946). Outlaws are robbing stages of valuable, government-insured money shipments and mail, then dispatching the vehicles with their dead drivers into a graveyard of deep water. Going into action against such treachery are postal inspectors Sunset Carson and Tom London, receiving aid from undercover Pinkerton detective Peggy Stewart. The trio's paths unmask express office manager Ted Adams after he silences cohort Kenne Duncan with a bullet. Adams, as renegade leader, is then gunned down by Carson at conclusion of this excellent action-oriented mystery tale. Sunset uses his bullwhip the last time here upon lashing female lead Stewart off her horse with a quick horseback segment.

RIO GRANDE RAIDERS (Republic, 1946). President Herbert Yates may have canned Sunset Carson, but before leaving the Republic lot permanently, the movie cowboy was put into a slam bang, superb B-Western full of action satisfying any viewer's appetite. Carson has brother problems again — this time it's Bob Steele in one of his best character roles after completely abandoning stardom in lensing low-budget oaters at the end of December 1945 with Producers Releasing Corporation (PRC). As an ex-convict forced to be in league with crooked stageline owner Tristram Coffin, craving rival Edmund Cobb's business, Steele has the threat of a shotgun man constantly pointing a gun at his back. Steele is tricked into a new holdup plus driving the Coffin stagecoach in a competitive race for the rival mail contract. Once Sunset's brother is plugged fatally, Carson avenges Steele's passing by shooting both the shotgunner and Coffin. Despite such script tenseness, a number of brief seconds are allowed for Bob Steele to have a hint of romance with leading lady Linda Stirling.

SUNSET CARSON RIDES AGAIN (Yucca, 1947 [Color]). What he thought would be a revival of his once promising B-Western career after the Republic ouster, Sunset Carson connected to producer Walt Mattox's Yucca Pictures, a small, cheap movie outfit about nine months later. Carson was to do only four with Mattox, and they would be weighted down with lots of negatives. Each one was in color, but the features were to be shot in 16mm and later enlarged to 35mm being grainy and out of focus for scattered movie theater distribution. Other drawbacks were too many amateur actors with too few professionals, bad film sound, sloppy sound effects, poor scripting and a mediocre music group. All these Westerns were to be directed by veteran Oliver Drake, not in true form with any of them. However, Sunset Carson looks sharply dressed for several segments with his Yucca debut on horse Cactus Jr. — the mount wouldn't receive any billing on-screen until BATTLING MARSHAL (Yucca, 1950) — in all-black, white pin-striped cowboy duds plus his great looking two-gun holster from the Republic days. Carson ranch partner, the always mean John Cason, but here cast with the first name of Bob, seeks to steal future funds for school construction while Sunset can't figure out young Al Terry's motives for suspecting him of deliberately killing Terry's father. After a boxing match is staged between Terry and Cason, Cason's men ambush Carson, who rallies to recover the stolen money and whip his nemesis in a river bed. This blah B-Western vehicle was not a good start for Sunset Carson with Mattox's set-up. Songs, including instrumentals, were "Prairie Wind," "Paradise Trail," "Pop Goes the Weasel," and "Listen to the Mockingbird."

FIGHTING MUSTANG (Yucca, 1948 [Color]). Horse thieves under leader Stephen Keyes operate from what appears as an impregnable outlaw territory that the state of Texas wants annexed via peoples' vote to restore much needed law and order. Texas Ranger Sunset Carson first has to deal with anxieties of neophyte lawman Al Terry trying to save a wild horse ordered destroyed for accidentally killing another Ranger. Action segments with standard Frank Sanucci music scoring go nowhere in this very poor horse tale. Even the annexation plot is reduced to a few seconds of production time. Sunset's movie efforts were fast sinking under Walt Mattox. Songs heard are "Happy Go-Lucky Buckaroos," "I'm a Lucky Son of a Gun," "Single I Am and Single I'll Stay," and "Blue Tail Fly."

DEADLINE (Yucca, 1948 [Color]). Sunset Carson rides, rides, and rides endlessly along with actress Pat Starling and others in this hollow saga of attempts to Frank Sanucci's scoring by a construction company to fulfill its Western Union contract to complete the telegraph line. Only crooked rancher Pat

Gleason wants the franchise for himself, and sets his gunmen under Stephen Keyes' guidance to attack the building efforts. Too much time is consumed in routine construction footage as well as the Carson/Starling horseback segments to pad out this production's length. The famous trio name of Russell, Majors, and Waddell is in error on building signs as two of the persons are misspelled "Russel" and "Waddel". Sunset's small one-gun holster contains no bullets which limits him to firing just two shots within the helter-skelter action footage. One song is "Way Out On the Prairie."

BATTLING MARSHAL (Yucca, 1950 [Color]). With Frank Sanucci gone from the credits, Al Corelli is his music score successor, and the results are atrocious which drag down this B-Western feature to the very bottom rung. Sunset Carson brought his abbreviated Yucca Pictures on the cinema trail to an end with Walt Mattox here in this ho-hum effort of shyster attorney Pat Gleason and gunslingers trying to frighten elderly rancher Jack Baxley from his property via a smallpox scare because a new vein has been discovered in the gold mine. Carson and sidekick Lee Roberts are weak in wiping away the Gleason gang with a so-so pace as U. S. Marshals. One funny scene has a gunman thinking he's out of ammo when the weapon accidentally fires a bullet. Reverse photography stock footage can be seen from Carson's FIGHTING MUSTANG (Yucca, 1948). Songs here are "Weep No More My Lady," "A Bird In a Gilded Cage," and "Searching Winds."

RIO GRANDE (Lautem, 1949). There were no more B-Westerns for Sunset Carson after he did this awful dog in Juanita, Texas. It's ghastly from start to finish with poor black/white photography, inept acting except from player Lee Morgan, a wretched screenplay, atrocious sound effects, and bad background music. Even interiors for the saloon and a bedroom were dirty looking and shabby. For what it's worth, Carson becomes involved in a waterhole dispute that finds rancher Bobby Clark accused of murder. Songs heard only in an unedited print are "Tonight's the Night" and "Ensenada".

A great latter-years pose by Sunset Carson intermingled among publicity material for his 1940s Republic and Yucca B-Westerns.

GOODBYE, SUNSET

Article from the *Knoxville News-Sentinel,* May 2, 1990

(Bear in mind that some details in these two obituaries are incorrect — his age and the number of movies, for instance.)

Reno, Nev. — Sunset Carson, a 1940s movie cowboy, died in Reno on Tuesday, one day after winning a settlement in a 3-year lawsuit over money earned from some of his old pictures.

Mr. Carson (63), died at Washoe Medical Center after apparently suffering a heart attack in his room at the Ponderosa Hotel. (Note: Sunset was 69 at the time of death.)

He was scheduled to be buried in Jackson, Tenn., where he had lived since 1988, said Jack Smith, of George A. Smith and Sons funeral parlor in Jackson.

Mr. Carson, who was a rodeo star at 17, appeared in nearly 40 Westerns including BANDITS OF THE BADLANDS, OREGON TRAIL, and BELLS OF ROSARITA.

In 1978, he put together a series of 78 classic Westerns featuring himself and other Western stars, including Ken Maynard and Roy Rogers.

He filed suit in 1987 complaining that South Carolina Educational Television Producers, Inc., and Ken Heard Releasing, Inc., helped in the production of the "Six Gun Heroes" but failed to pay him for videocassette sales and promotional material sold on the show since 1982.

Mr. Carson's Reno attorney, Larry Dunn, said the suit was settled out of court in Mr. Carson's favor on Monday. Dunn would not give a money amount.

Mr. Carson spent recent years crusading against drugs, violence, sex, and crude language in movies and television.

He is survived by his wife of one year, Jeanne, a son, and a daughter.

Article from the *Atlanta Journal,* May 2, 1990

You know the old Buddhist riddle: What is the sound of one hand clapping? Well, a 1940's cowboy movie star, Sunset Carson, died this week in Reno, Nev. He was 63 and had appeared in more than 40 Westerns, stuff like BANDITS OF THE BADLANDS, OREGON TRAIL and BELLS OF ROSARITA.

Hmmmm. When Sunset dies, what's left for him to ride off into?
We live in complicated times.
Yippee-i-ay.

Don Key and grandson Nathan at Sunset's gravesite in Jackson, Tennessee.

PHOTO GALLERY

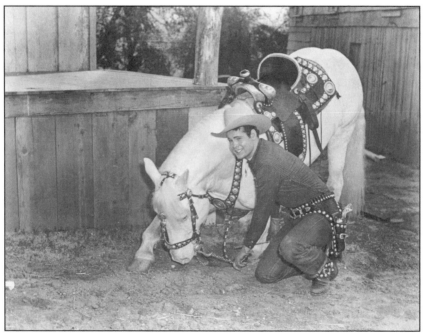

Sunset has horse Silver take a bow on the Republic lot.

Taking a Republic camera break, Sunset rests on Silver.

Another Republic pose for Sunset and Silver.

Sunset and Silver at Republic's Duchess Ranch set.

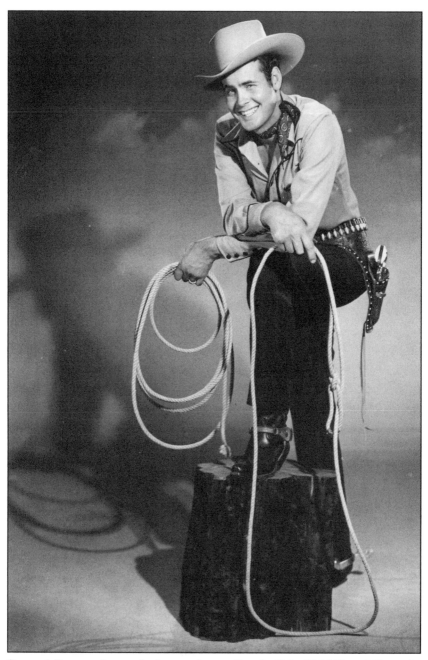

Sunset Carson is ready for roping action in this 1944 Republic publicity shot.

While shooting SHERIFF OF CIMARRON (Republic, 1945), Sunset poses with guns drawn.

Sunset looks for gold-bullion thieves on horse Silver in SHERIFF OF CIMARRON (Republic, 1945.)

A 1946 Sunset publicity photo at Republic.

Sunset in 1946 on the Republic back lot.

"So long, Pardners."

SELECTED BIBLIOGRAPHY

Anderson, Chuck, The Old Corral website.

Carman, Bob and Scapperotti, Dan, *The Western Films of Sunset Carson* (Robert C. Carman, 1981).

Copeland, Bobby J., *Trail Talk* (Empire Publishing, 1996).

Copeland, Bobby J., *B-Western Boot Hill* (Empire Publishing, 1999).

Drake, Oliver, *Written, Produced and Directed By Oliver Drake* (The Outlaw Press, 1990).

Horwitz, James, *They Went Thataway* (Thomas Congdon Books,1976).

Magers, Boyd, *Western Clippings* (various issues).

Momber, Colin, *Wrangler's Roost* (various issues).

Mathis, Jack, *Republic Confidential, Volume 2, The Players* (Jack Mathis Advertising, 1992).

Miller, Don, *Hollywood Corral* (Popular Library Publishers, 1976).

McCord, Merrill, *Brothers of the West — The Lives and Films of Robert Livingston and Jack Randall* (Alhambra Publications, 2003).

Rothel, David, *Those Great Cowboy Sidekicks* (WOY Publications, 1984).

ABOUT THE AUTHORS

Reared in Oak Ridge, Tennessee, Bobby Copeland began going to the Saturday matinee B-Western movies at nearby theaters. He was immediately impressed by the moral code of these films and has tried to pattern his life after the examples set by the cowboy heroes. After graduating from high school and attending Carson-Newman College and the University of Tennessee, he set out to raise a family and start a career at the Oak Ridge National Laboratory. His love for the old Western films was put on the shelf and lay dormant for some 35 years. One Saturday, in the mid-1980s, he happened to turn on his television, and the station was showing a Lash LaRue movie. This rekindled his interest. He contacted the TV program's host ("Marshal" Andy Smalls) and was invited to appear on the program. Since that time, Bobby has had some 100 articles published, written 12 books, contributed to some 20 books, made several speeches, appeared on television over 40 times, and has been interviewed by several newspapers and four independent radio stations as well as the Public Radio Broadcasting System to provide commentary and promote interest in B-Western films. In 1985 he was a co-founder of the Knoxville, Tennessee-based "Riders of the Silver Screen Club," serving five times as president. He initiated and edited the club's newsletter for several years.

In 1996, Bobby's first book, *Trail Talk*, was published by Empire Publishing, Inc. (one of the world's largest publishers of books on Western films and performers). It was followed by *B-Western Boot Hill, Bill Elliott — The Peaceable Man, Roy Barcroft — King of the Badmen, Charlie King — We Called Him Blackie, Silent Hoofbeats, Johnny Mack Brown — Up Close and Personal, Sunset Carson — The Adventures of a Cowboy Hero,* and *Best of the Badmen* by Boyd Magers, Bob Nareau, and Bobby. In addition to these popular books, Bobby also self-published *The Bob Baker Story, The Whip Wilson Story,* and *Five Heroes.* He has attended some 60

Western film festivals, and has met many of the Western movie performers. He continues to contribute articles to the various Western magazines, and he is a regular columnist for *Western Clippings*. In 1988, Bobby received the "Buck Jones Rangers Trophy," presented annually to individuals demonstrating consistent dedication to keeping the spirit of the B-Western alive. In 1994, Don Key (Empire Publishing) and Boyd Magers (Video West, Inc. & *Western Clippings*) awarded Bobby the "Buck Rainey Shoot-em-Ups Pioneer Award," which yearly honors a fan who has made significant contributions towards the preservation of interest in the B-Westerns. In 2006, he received the "Saddle Pal Award," presented by the *Old Cowboy Picture Show* Magazine, and in 2007, he was honored with the "Edward A. Wall Memorial Award" by the Williamsburg Film Festival. Bobby has been featured on two DVDs — one about the history of B-Western films, and another about the life of Dub Taylor.

Bobby is an active member at Oak Ridge's Central Baptist Church. He retired in 1996 after 40 years at the same workplace. Bobby plans to continue his church work, write more B-Western articles, and enjoy his retirement with his faithful sidekick, Joan.

Bobby and Joan Copeland enjoy a laugh with Sunset Carson at the 1986 Knoxville Western Film Caravan.

Richard B. Smith, III is a retired writer and editor whose devotion to the B-Western genre began around 1949 when at age 8 he made occasional Saturday-matinee visits to see Gene Autry and Roy Rogers in their musical horse operas at the small Pitts-Clarco Theater in Berryville, Virginia. Further knowledge for young Richard about these features accelerated by the time he saw old B-Westerns simultaneously on television beginning in August 1951.

In 1958, Smith commenced serious research for film credits on shoot-em-up stars by constantly perusing old movie display ads from newspaper morgues of northwestern Virginia and far eastern West Virginia. Over the last four decades, he has scanned film books, files and trade papers such as *Variety* and *The Hollywood Reporter* at the Library of Congress.

Richard worked for the late Jack Mathis (from 1980 to 1982) whose "Republic Confidential" project required him to compile a super-index of credits on Republic Pictures (1935-1959) players and technical personnel which was done from October 2, 1980 through April 21, 1981 over a 202-day period. For Mathis, he also photo copied 25 years of *Variety* microfilm articles on Republic plus assembled a trade papers compendium. Smith's uncredited work was published in two Mathis books — *Republic Confidential (Vol. 1 —The Studio, 1999 and Vol. 2 — The Players, 1992).*

Richard authored "B-Westerns in Perspective" beginning in 1978 for *The Big Reel,* then as a separate publication and later during 1989 for *Under Western Skies*, with each highlighted movie having data on filming dates, locations, production criteria, etc. He also contributed the same format in columns for *Western Clippings* (1994-2002) titled "Behind the Cameras."

Smith was co-author with John Rutherford on *Cowboy Shooting Stars* (1988) and on the expanded *More Cowboy Shooting Stars* (1992).

During 2006-2007, Richard was editorial assistant on Boyd Magers' *Gene Autry Westerns* (2007). He also offered editorial assistance on former B-Western actor House Peters, Jr.'s autobiography, *Another Side of Hollywood* (2001) and Merrill McCord's *Brothers of the West: The Lives and Films of Robert Livingston and Jack Randall* (2003).

In recent years, Richard has lent editorial help also on prolific writer Bobby Copeland's many publications: *The Bob Baker Story, The Whip Wilson Story, Five Heroes* (all in 1998), *B-Western Boot Hill* (1999), *Bill Elliott — The Peaceable Man* (2000), *Roy Barcroft — King of the Badmen* (2000), *Silent Hoof-*

Richard B. Smith, III

beats (2001), *Charlie King — We Called Him Blackie* (2003), and *Johnny Mack Brown — Up Close and Personal* (2005). In 1999, Richard was the 9th and last recipient of the "Buck Rainey Shoot-Em-Ups Pioneer Award" which recognized his literary contributions.

Smith is a 1963 B.A. graduate of Shepherd University, Shepherdstown, West Virginia, having majored in English with a minor in Journalism.

Other Fine Western Books Available from Empire Publishing, Inc:

ABC's of Movie Cowboys by Edgar M. Wyatt. $5.00.

Art Acord and the Movies by Grange B. McKinney. $15.00.

Audie Murphy: Now Showing by Sue Gossett. $30.00.

Back in the Saddle: Essays on Western Film and Television Actors edited by Garry Yoggy. $29.95.

Best of the Badmen by Boyd Magers, Bobby Copeland, and Bob Nareau. $39.00.

Bill Elliott, The Peaceable Man by Bobby Copeland. $15.00.

Brothers of the West: The Lives and Films of Robert Livingston and Jack Randall by Merrill McCord. $34.95.

B-Western Boot Hill: A Final Tribute to the Cowboys and Cowgirls Who Rode the Saturday Matinee Movie Range by Bobby Copeland

B-Western Actors Encyclopedia by Ted Holland. $30.00.

Buster Crabbe, A Self-Portrait as told to Karl Whitezel. $24.95.

B-Western Boot Hill: A Final Tribute to the Cowboys and Cowgirls Who Rode the Saturday Matinee Movie Range by Bobby Copeland. $15.00.

Charlie King: We Called Him Blackie by Bobby Copeland. $15.00.

The Cowboy and the Kid by Jefferson Brim Crow, III. $5.90.

Crusaders of the Sagebrush by Hank Williams. $29.95.

Duke, The Life and Image of John Wayne by Ronald L. Davis. $14.95.

The Films and Career of Audie Murphy by Sue Gossett. $18.00.

The First Fifty Years of Sound Western Movie Locations by Kenny Stier. $34.95.

Gene Autry Westerns — America's Favorite Cowboy by Boyd Magers. $45.00.

The Golden Corral, A Roundup of Magnificent Western Films by Ed Andreychuk. $29.95.

The Hollywood Posse, The Story of a Gallant Band of Horsemen Who Made Movie History by Diana Serra Cary. $16.95.

Hoppy by Hank Williams. $29.95.

In a Door, Into a Fight, Out a Door, Into a Chase, Movie-Making Remembered by the Guy at the Door by William Witney. $24.95.

John Ford, Hollywood's Old Master by Ronald L. Davis. $14.95.

John Wayne—Actor, Artist, Hero by Richard D. McGhee. $27.50.

John Wayne, An American Legend by Roger M. Crowley. $29.95.

Johnny Mack Brown—Up Close and Personal by Bobby Copeland. $20.00.

Kid Kowboys: Juveniles in Western Films by Bob Nareau. $20.00.

Ask for our complete listing of WESTERN MOVIE BOOKS!

Ladies of the Western by Boyd Magers and Michael G. Fitzgerald. $35.00.

Lash LaRue, King of the Bullwhip by Chuck Thornton and David Rothel. $25.00.

Last of the Cowboy Heroes by Budd Boetticher. $28.50.

More Cowboy Shooting Stars by John A. Rutherford and Richard B. Smith, III. $18.00.

The Official TV Western Roundup Book by Neil Summers and Roger M. Crowley. $34.95.

Randolph Scott, A Film Biography by Jefferson Brim Crow, III. $25.00.

Richard Boone: A Knight Without Armor in a Savage Land by David Rothel. $30.00.

Riding the (Silver Screen) Range, The Ultimate Western Movie Trivia Book by Ann Snuggs. $15.00.

Riding the Video Range, The Rise and Fall of the Western on Television by Garry A. Yoggy. $75.00.

The Round-Up, A Pictorial History of Western Movie and Television Stars Through the Years by Donald R. Key. $27.00.

Roy Rogers, A Biography, Radio History, Television Career Chronicle, Discography, Filmography, etc. by Robert W. Phillips. $75.00.

Roy Barcroft: King of the Badmen by Bobby Copeland. $15.00.

The Roy Rogers Reference-Trivia-Scrapbook by David Rothel. $25.00.

Saddle Gals, A Filmography of Female Players in B-Westerns of the Sound Era by Edgar M. Wyatt and Steve Turner. $10.00.

Silent Hoofbeats: A Salute to the Horses and Riders of the Bygone B-Western Era by Bobby Copeland. $20.00.

Singing in the Saddle by Douglas B. Green. $34.95.

Sixty Great Cowboy Movie Posters by Bruce Hershenson. $14.99.

Smiley Burnette: We Called Him Frog by Bobby J. Copeland and Richard B. Smith, III. $18.00.

The Sons of the Pioneers by Bill O'Neal and Fred Goodwin. $26.95.

So You Wanna See Cowboy Stuff? by Boyd Magers. $25.00.

Tex Ritter: America's Most Beloved Cowboy by Bill O'Neal. $21.95.

Those Great Cowboy Sidekicks by David Rothel. $25.00.

Trail Talk, Candid Comments and Quotes by Performers and Participants of The Saturday Matinee Western Films by Bobby Copeland. $12.50.

The Western Films of Sunset Carson by Bob Carman and Dan Scapperotti. $20.00.

Western Movies: A TV and Video Guide to 4200 Genre Films compiled by Michael R. Pitts. $35.00.

Westerns Women by Boyd Magers and Michael G. Fitzgerald. $35.00.

Written, Produced, and Directed by Oliver Drake. $30.00.

Add $4.00 shipping/handling for first book + $1.00 for each additional book ordered.

Empire Publishing, Inc. • **3130 US Highway 220** • **Madison, NC 27025-8306** • **Phone 336-427-5850**